LIFE AFTER ART SCHOOL

Copyright © 2021 by Mark Zajac

All rights reserved. This book or any portion thereof may not be reproduced or used in any manner whatsoever without the express written permission of the publisher except for the use of brief quotations in a book review.

Printed in the United States of America

First Printing, 2021

Piggyback Press
www.piggybackpress.com

Life After Art School

101 Fun Size Lessons of Adulting
For Artists or Anyone That
Wants To Level Up

Mark Zajac

PIGGYBACK PRESS

Dedicated to all the courageous people who decided to zag instead of zig, and despite everyone's advice, went to art school.

Table of Contents

1. College is Over Priced 1
2. Art Schools are Pretentious 3
3. Overconfidence Kills 5
4. Always Be Kind.. 7
5. Don't Look for Insults.. 9
6. Art is a Business... 11
7. Get Out of Your Lane... 13
8. Stop Romanticizing Art 15
9. Selling Out 17
10. Do Art for the Sake of It... 19
11. The Genius Myth 21
12. Embrace a Growth Mindset 23
13. Who Moved Your Cheese? 25
14. Solving the Right Problem 27
15. All Nighters Suck.. 29
16. You Don't Have to Be a Fast Learner 31
17. Be Humble... 33
18. It's All About the Journey 35
19. We're All in Sales, Kid.. 37
20. The Kaizen Method 39
21. What's Phubbing?.. 41
22. The Illusion of Multitasking... 43
23. Fight for Your Right to Concentrate!....................................... 45
24. Immediacy Does Not Equal Importance 47
25. Learn How to Concentrate 49
26. Learn to Eat Your Frogs 51
27. Shiny Objects 53
28. Learn to Network 55
29. Surround Yourself with Smart People..................................... 57
30. Feature Creep 59
31. 3X. 61
32. Free Exposure.. 63
33. Learning To Say NO 65
34. Be the Right Candidate... 67

35. Interview the Interviewer 69
36. How You Do One Thing... 71
37. Macs are Useless in the Corporate World 73
38. Tailor Your Resume 75
39. The Briefcase Method 77
40. Jobs are the Riskiest Investments 79
41. Your Job is Your Patron 81
42. Clients not Customers 83
43. Find Beauty in the Ordinary 85
44. The Good, the Bad, and the Ugly in Design 87
45. When People Zig, Zag 89
46. Time is on Your Side When it Comes to This 91
47. It's OK to Ask For Help 93
48. One Reason Why You Should Teach Someone 95
49. Learn to Take an Existential Punch 97
50. But Don't Be a Punching Bag 99
51. Within Structure Thrives Creativity 101
52. Look to Serve 103
53. Don't Fake It Til You Make It. Do This Instead 105
54. Passive Income as an Artist 107
55. Time is Money but Money is NEVER Time 109
56. Find Time 111
57. Embrace the Present Moment 113
58. Why You Should Learn Marketing 115
59. What is Brand 117
60. Why Reading is Not Enough 119
61. Design With the Customer in Mind 121
62. Sharing is Caring 123
63. Please Learn Typography 125
64. The Starving Artist Myth 127
65. The Attitude of Gratitude 129
66. Don't Vilify the Wealthy 131
67. Effective is More Important Than Pretty 133
68. The Oppression of Choice 135
69. The Psychology of Color 137
70. Read the Opposite of What You Believe 139
71. Shadow Someone for the Day 141

72. Don't Try to be Everything to Everyone 143
73. Live Within Your Means but Don't be a Martyr About it 145
74. Don't Get Eaten by Sharks 147
75. Happiness According to a Greek Philosopher 149
76. Do Hard Things 151
77. What We Overestimate and Underestimate 153
78. Learn How to Brainstorm 155
79. Solve the Right Problem 157
80. w * 5 = n 159
81. Learn to Stress Out 161
82. To Resolute or Not Resolute? 163
83. Give Credit Where Credit's Due 165
84. The War of Art 167
85. Don't Wait for Inspiration 169
86. The Spirit of the Amateur 171
87. Redefine Wealth 173
88. Get Over Your Hangups with Money 175
89. Charismatic Lives Matter 177
90. No One is Coming to Save You 179
91. The World Doesn't Owe You Anything 181
92. Listen Up 183
93. Become Worth Following 185
94. Distraction or Traction 187
95. Learned Helplessness 189
96. Are Pictures Better Than Words? 191
97. Maturity 193
98. The Marshmallow Test 195
99. Learn How to See, Learn How to Speak 197
100. Get to the Next Barrel 199
101. Becoming a Master 201

Introduction

THIS IS NOT A GREAT BOOK. Sorry to disappoint you if you thought otherwise. Don't get me wrong, it's not a terrible book either. It's just a simple little book that hopefully, at the end, leaves you heading in a number of right directions. So keep this in mind. Small changes that you apply early can lead to massive gains way down the road of life.

As one of those "creative types," I went to school for art and was lucky enough to later eck out a living, both as a "sometimes[1]" artist and as a full time graphic designer. Besides art and design, personal development has always been important to me. I've read a lot of books and wrecked many a notebook.

From my successes, failures and all of my ' holy crap, what the hell was I thinking!' moments, I was able to pick up some useful gems of experience and knowledge. What I found useful and –hopefully you will too– I wanted to keep for myself and distilled conveniently into one place. And that's how I created this little, "not-that-great-but-perhaps-good- and-useful-lil-book."

You don't have to take me or this book all too seriously[2], all I ask is that you give me and it a chance and that you explore the topics and to refer to the actual experts in the field. Not all of the chapters are going to resonate with you and that's OK. You're also going to disagree with me on occasion too and that's also OK. You might even get triggered, send me a scathing email and leave me a terrible review which is not OK. Please don't do that.

This concludes the Introduction portion of the book. Aren't book introductions just the worst?

---

1 Something I would say when someone asked me if I was an artist. Usually I'd say 'sometimes.'
2 Well, you can take me a little seriously.

1
College is Over Priced

But I don't have to tell you that! I'll, however, break this to you. Most likely your school didn't teach you shit. Maybe it taught you some shit but it's not close to the shit of what adulting will be like for the next 50 some odd years. In other words, if you've graduated, your *real* education is about to begin. Welcome to the jungle, Kevin.

If school taught you anything, if it was only one thing that would really matter for the rest of your life, it would be to learn how to learn. School wasn't the end, it was only the syllabus.

It's my prediction, along with many others, that employers will stop putting so much precedence on education and much more on attitude and mindset. This is the correct indicator by the way since a diploma is not necessary in becoming a good employee.

Don't get me wrong, I'm not resentful towards higher education. I loved college but with the high price tag of education today you have to make a cost/benefit analysis of your investment. In other words, is the juice worth the squeeze?

Art Schools are Pretentious

LET'S FACE IT, art schools can be damn pretentious. We read a few books, take a few classes, throw a few ten dollar words into our conversations and all of a sudden we have fallen for what is known as the "Illusion of Mastery." That's just an academic term meaning we think we're pretty hot shit. Don't worry, it's not you. We've all fallen for it.

Here's the antidote. Be humble. Even when you know a lot you say? Especially when you know a lot. Because when you think you know a lot, actually you really don't. At least you can agree there's always much much more to know.

We all need to keep ourselves in check but here's the thing. I have never heard an actual master of his/her craft say they have mastered their craft. Because the more they do, the more they want to explore. Their journey of learning is never over.

Fact: You don't have it all figured out yet and that's perfectly OK. It's not a Millennial thing, every generation thought they were hot shit. Some more than others. Cough cough Boomers cough.

Pretending to be a master when you're not really does the opposite of what you intend. It shows insecurity. What would be a better choice? Be open to ideas and look at the world with curious eyes. You're an artist for God's Sake! Everyone has a unique perspective on the world so don't discount anyone at face value. Which segways nicely to the next page...

3
Overconfidence Kills

Literally. I was introduced to woodworking when I approached a woodworking friend of mine and asked if he would teach me how to use a lathe. At the time I wanted to make my own baseball bat.[1] After his introduction, I couldn't wait to get started. He just had one more bit of advice for me...

"Before you start, let me just say that tools don't change but your attitude towards them does." He noticed I had my usual perplexed look on my face so he went on.

"In other words, it's not a beginner that gets hurt, usually they are intimidated by the machine. It's only when that beginner gains confidence quickly[2], perhaps too much confidence, too quickly because they start to take the dangers for granted. And that's when bad stuff happens."

It's good to be confident. Confidence allows us to try new things and move us past our comfort zones. But confidence should never replace the respect for the craft, the tools you are using and how possibly dangerous it could all be.

---

1 *By the way, not as easy as you might expect.*
2 *The Mastery of Illusion thang.*

4
Always Be Kind

I'M CONVINCED THAT empathy is something we build over time. Maybe it's through experience; knowing what it's like to be knocked around a few times. And once we see someone go through the same experience, it just might activate our empathy-making machines.

It's easy to be critical. There's a lot to be critical about if you look for it hard enough. If someone isn't playing by the rules, especially our rules, then we tend to want to call them out on it.

The best way, (and by no means the easiest way) is to traverse this life without looking for insults. The persons that aren't playing by the rules could very well be fighting some hard, internal battles. Or maybe they could just be an asshole.

> *"Be kind, for everyone you meet is fighting a hard battle."*
>
> — Lots of great people although I first read this quote in Bob Dylan's Autobiography.

5
Don't Look for Insults

ANGER CAN DESTROY your day. It has for me and trust me I live where the anger runs deep. But remember, we decide what to feel and anger is an easy one to get to. Looking to be offended can put you in a pissy mood. Is our pissiness justified? Probably. There are plenty of terrible things to get upset about. But that isn't the problem. There's always something to be angry about. The world is full of examples to find.

The challenge is not to justify an action to feel angry. You have every right to feel angry if someone cuts you off in traffic. It's what we decide to do with that anger that matters.

Take a road rage case. Our immediate reaction is to react with rage when a possibly dangerous scenario happens before us. But before you react with hostility, think about what that driver is possibly going through. Perhaps they just found out their father is in the emergency room suffering from a massive heart attack. Now it still doesn't excuse them from driving recklessly but you're more willing to cut them some slack. You don't know the whole story. So why come up with the worse possible scenario?

This is known as Cognitive Reframing and it's a great tool to have in your toolbox. You're better off reframing the reality and while you're at it, create it for the benefit of your emotional state.

Tip: Raise your vibration by remembering a time when your vibration was really high or you can make one up. What would it feel like to win the lottery? Or when you kissed that girl or guy you had a crush on? These states can raise your vibration high enough where nothing or no one would have the ability to knock you off your good vibes.

Deep Dive:
"The Charisma Myth" by Olivia Fox Cabane

6
Art is a Business

IT CERTAINLY IS AND we make art to sell art so we can make more art. But like with all businesses, in order to sustain ourselves, we have to make a profit. And profits come when you have something the market demands.

I remember a friend of a friend who sold paintings (I mean tried to sell paintings?) at art festivals. Selling wasn't really her forte and this friend of a friend didn't do very well. Whenever we saw her at the end of a long day at a festival, let's just say the conversation wasn't very positive. To be brutally honest, (And I will promise you, I will be brutally honest) I didn't like her paintings and I would never have bought one at the prices she was charging. Yes I'm being subjective but since she wasn't selling anything, I had a feeling that I wasn't the only one. It's just the hard truth.

My friend would mention how the art business wasn't being kind to her. My knee-jerk reaction was to say, 'Well, maybe she should paint something people would want to buy.' Sounds insensitive but it's also simple business sense[3]. Naturally, my friend was taken aback by my brutal, jerky honesty, even if she might have thought the same. We never got to give her any feedback and to our defense, she never asked. But it's real talk to admit that yes, you're an artist and yes, you're in business. So start thinking business-ee!

The simple magic of making art that sells:
1. Make something people would want to buy. Find a niche!
2. Do it well. Practice and get good at your craft[4].
3. Be unique and bring something new and exciting to the table. A new

---
[3] *Remember it's good to be honest but it's also good to be kind. Toggling between the two take a lot of tact. Trust me I know.*
[4] *Sorry I meant art.*

perspective, your wonderful and inspiring perspective! Voila!

Hey, I said it was simple, not easy.

Remember it's good to be honest but it's also good to be kind. Toggling between the two take a lot of tact. Trust me I know.

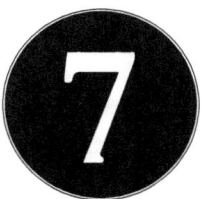

Get Out of Your Lane

ARTISTS WANT TO DO art things. I get it. But experiencing something new helps you develop fresh perspectives. My path towards the "new" started when I experienced some mid-career burnout as a freelance graphic designer. One day while visiting a local community college (actually the college where I had my first art classes, long long ago), I saw a sign advertising a new Organic Agriculture program. That week I signed up[5].

Now maybe you don't have to go to that extreme (or maybe you should!). But for me, doing the "opposite" or simply something radically different did three things:

1) It gave me a new appreciation for what I did and do now. Who would have thunk it but I really like sitting down. And heat. Heat is soooo nice in the winter and air conditioning in the Summer. Fantastic!

2) It gave me an opportunity to use my skills to serve people I would not have met otherwise.

3) It opened up so many fresh perspectives on life and the world, I would not have gained if I stayed in my lane.

Moral of the story: You don't have to join the foreign legion or the Peace Corps to briefly step outside of your world and into a new one. But try doing something you wouldn't normally do and you just might be surprised how enlightening and refreshing it can be.

---

5 And, yadda yadda yadda because of those courses, I ended up in Jamaica as a Peace Corps volunteer but that's another story.

8

Stop Romanticizing Art

WE ALL HAVE DONE it, haven't we? And why not? These characters from art history become "larger than life" as mere students and the masterpieces they created seem to have come from another world. These masters appeared to be immortal-like beings destined to grace us with their sacred genius. And it's all bullshit. Yep. The truth is they were simply tough, hard-working entrepreneurs that did it for the money. Yep. The Leonardos, the Michelangelos, and the Raphaels all had to get paid.

As Austin Kleon, author of the book, "Show Your Work" has said, "Some of the most meaningful and cherished cultural artifacts were made for money." Which makes art a business. This leads nicely to the next point and what art students have been dealing with for a millennia. Go ahead, flip the page...

Deep Dive:
   "Show your Work" by Austin Kleon

9
Selling Out

Ah, the ol "selling out" debate. Every art student has faced it. Sometimes the topic becomes so insidious, there are even schisms between art majors. Back in my day, it was the fine art students like the painters, printmakers, and sculptures that accused the commercial artists, us graphic designers, of "selling out." "You're prostituting yourself!" they would say. "You're just doing it for the money!" they would say. Well, guess what, they're right. But in case you didn't know, we're all doing it for the money.

There's another term for "selling out." It's called being successful. And it's funny how we as a fan can come to cherish artists when they're starting out only to turn on them when they become popular and successful. Everyone has the right to explore, pivot, experiment, evolve and change. Is it jealousy or is it because we like our muses to stay within a box of what they are suppose to be in our heads. Either way, it's selfish for us to put limits on the people we admire.

So please don't do that. And if you're one of those lucky persons who does get a healthy slice of success and ends up making it big, please remember it was this little book of rants from a grumpy middle-aged artist that gave you the edge and insight to get you there.

If you got something worthy to sell and you're "selling out," the people that ain't selling shit might just be the ones throwing that accusation around all too loosely. Enjoy your success and DO NOT feel guilty or let anyone bring you down for it[6].

---

6 Unless you lied, cheated, and stolen to get there. If that's the case, please feel free to feel guilty.

10
Do Art for the Sake of It

AND NOW FOR something completely different[7]. Flying in the face of what I just said, you know that whole, art is a business thing. Yay for contradictions!

Go ahead and make art for the fun of it. Make it pretty or ugly, controversial, or whatever your heart desires. Art is a wonderful form of self-expression and by all means, express your wild freaky self. But just because you dig what your doing, don't assume everyone else is going to too. It's great when these two align perfectly but it's also rare[8].

---

[7] *Monty Python's Flying Circus reference if you're not in the know.*
[8] *The friend of a friend I mentioned on the previous page got these mixed up.*

11

The Genius Myth

WE ALL HAVE OUR HEROES. You know, the people we admire and lean to for inspiration. Many of them have been labeled geniuses and maybe rightfully so, I mean sure, they were masters at what they did. Names like Da Vinci, Michelangelo, Van Gogh and Picasso are easily associated and described as genius. And trust me, it's easy as artists to immortalize these guys. But this whole genius pedestal thing can get carried away pretty quick[9].

Here's the straight dope. Genius is nothing more than hard work executed over a consistent amount of time. Sure talent can matter, but talent by itself will get you nowhere if it isn't for the sweat equity and dedication. In short, geniuses aren't appointed from above, they are made down here on Earth.

Of course, no one is going to be offended if you call them a genius, and, by no surprise, I'm not expecting that title will be bestowed upon me anytime soon. But labeling someone a genius, especially early on in life, can cement what's known as a *fixed mindset*.

If only there was another, healthier mindset to nurture. Ah, but there is! Go ahead, flip the page. You know you want to.

---

[9] *Whenever you put someone on a pedestal, they now have the opportunity to look down on you.*

Embrace a Growth Mindset

WELL INTENDED GROWNUPS have said to me when I was a child, "Oh you're so talented![10]" Sure it was nice to hear, but the downside to being "talented" meant there was a lot of pressure to live up to. We're talented and talented people don't f**k up.

People who fall into the, "You either have it or you don't" camp have what is known as a fixed mindset. These people love their genius status but HATE to fail and have their title in question. This might be the reason why they shy away from new challenges. Failing might be evidence that they really don't possess that special sauce after all.

In comparison to the fixed mindset, a growth mindset puts all of the empathize on the work and the process. Similar to working out in a gym, putting in enough sweat equity will get you the results. The more you work at your craft, the better you're going to get. Full stop.

Deep Dive:
"Growth Mindset" by Carol Dewitt

---

10 *Let's face it, you were probably told that too.*

13

Who Moved Your Cheese?

Your dream job. You got it. Congratulations! But let me give you some controversial words of advice. Having a job, even a dreamy one, is the riskiest investment you can make. Whaaaat? Do you mean to tell me riskier than actually working for yourself? Yep. That's exactly what I'm telling you.

Your job is temporary. All jobs are temporary and not only are they temporary, but they are also unpredictable. Any job could end at any point at any time without warning. It doesn't matter how good the company is or how well they're doing. If the business your in is in business for profit, then they're what we call amoral. Not to be confused with what is moral or immoral, amoral means that businesses have one primary objective and that's profit.

So what's one to do in a capitalistic amoral society? Even if you have a job you like and you feel secure always always always work on yourself and your skills. Leverage that job you have now by building your skill sets and your portfolio. This will come in handy in your next position. And trust me, there will be multiple positions in your life. As Jim Rohn once said, "your income is based on your self-development."

Hope for the best, prepare for the worst. We all have heard it but how many people actually follow this little cliche' of neglected wisdom?

Deep Dive:
    Who Moved Your Cheese? by Dr. Spencer Johnson
    (This is a small quirky lil book but packs a punch of wisdom!)

Solving the Right Problem

RORY SUTHERLAND, IN my opinion, is a brilliant marketer[11]. If you ever read one of his books and I suggest that you do, he has one core underlining life lesson: spend your time and energy solving the right problem. Here's one of his examples.

People hate commuting to work. They especially dislike riding on commuter trains. If you interviewed one of these commuters, most likely they would wish their commute was shorter. If we were an engineer, the solution is simple. Make trains go faster. Engineering trains to run faster, however, would be expensive and also limiting. Trains can only go so fast safely. But why even go down that route in the first place? Perhaps we're solving the wrong problem.

The real problem isn't about speed, it's about the traveler's enjoyability. Instead of making the trains faster, why not try to make them more enjoyable? It's an easier problem to solve and far less expensive. In fact, if they were actually enjoyable, people would start complaining that their ride wasn't long enough!

Deep Dive:
  "Alchemy" by Rory Sutherland

---

11 *Like Seth Godin, he works in a good amount of behavioral economics into his marketing.*

15

All Nighters Suck

I don't know about you but I actually hated all-nighters when I was in school, mostly because they were so unnecessary.

Unnecessary? Yes, and you can blame them on a little-known thing called Parkinson's Law. This law states that "work expands so as to fill the time available for its completion." So if the project was due in two weeks on a Monday morning, one could easily predict what every art student would be working on their project at 1:00 am on a Sunday night. 'If only I had another week' you think to yourself in your sleepy delirium.

It makes you wonder that humans are terrible time managers. The evidence suggests we are. To avoid this, don't take time for granted. If we're given a generous amount of time to complete a project, don't procrastinate, start it[12].

And the way we can do this is to block out units of time. Breaking down a project into simple tasks makes the project look less daunting and more attractive to start. Manage your time well and finally get a good night's sleep.

---

12 Easier said than done I know!

16

You Don't Have to Be a Fast Learner

Hey if you're fast, you're fast. Good for you. But what's more important than picking up something quickly is learning smart. I like to call it, "just in time" learning.

Being a just-in-time learner means prioritizing your learning schedule. It's not about the speed or understanding it all at once but rather just learning what you need to know at that moment, taking it one little step by little step. Just enough to get you to the next step.

Here's an example. During the first wave of the pandemic, my past employer got us to start making video content for YouTube and I volunteered to edit the videos; a perfect opportunity to build my skill sets.

Now did I need to wait and be a master at After Effects and Premiere to start? Absolutely not. If you take it step by step, you don't have to rush your learning because you don't need to know it all to do a good job.

Here was my first baby step. Learn to open a video file, make a simple edit, close and save it in the format I needed. That's it. Within minutes I was now an official video editor. Win! Next, I needed to make an opening and a closing for all our video content. No problem, keep it simple. I managed to make a simple opening by animating a few objects and text and added a small clip of music. This went on, learning as I went from one project to the next steadily getting better along the way.

The moral? Don't wait to be "good." You get better through the process. And as you'll get to understand, you need to fall in love with the process. Have I mentioned it's all about the process?

17

Be Humble

Artists tend to think they are special unicorns and I'm here to try to put a stop to it even if it's a feeble one. It's wonderful to be in a profession where you get to be creative and make a good living from it. But we should never lose sight of our humility. Not only would it make us a more agreeable and all-around better human, but for our personal development as well. If you do take your personal development journey seriously, there are definite benefits to your daily dose of humble pie. Here are just a few:

Leadership. Admitting to your imperfections and mistakes is admired and respected. It shows genuineness and that you have integrity. Your team may not like a know-it-all but they can definitely relate to a boss that is willing to show their softer side. Leaders who are identified as humble are known to be more effective.

Better Relationships. I don't have to go off on a limb in saying that people that are considered humble are simply more agreeable. Also, when we own up to our fallibilities, this of course makes us more relatable, but it also transforms our mindset. A humble mindset allows us to be flexible, curious, inclusive, and open to new experiences.

Learning. We can drop the whole, I-know-it-all routine because that just isn't a good look for us. Thinking that we have to have the answer to everything is not only wrong, it can lead to embarrassing moments. Some of my favorite people are the most humble and often the smartest. And what smart people have in common is that they are great listeners, ask a lot of questions, and are genuinely curious about other people's experiences and the world around them.

"Humility is the true key to success. Successful people lose their way at times. They often embrace and overindulge from the fruits of success. Humility halts this arrogance and self-indulging trap. Humble people share the credit and wealth, remaining focused and hungry to continue the journey of success."

— Rick Pitino

18
It's All About the Journey

I HATE TO BREAK this to you but your happiness isn't lying around the corner. You won't feel complete once you get that dream job, buy that perfect house, get that beautiful wife/husband/above average children/etc. Although those things aren't terrible, we equate them with our own internal happiness. It's the proverbial carrot that gives us the reason to keep us constantly chasing happiness just around the corner.

It's essential to have goals. But the key is to enjoy the journey; all the journeys to your goals.

Deep Dive:
There's no other person that really can sum this up better than Sir Alan Watts. There are many lectures that were recorded and uploaded on YouTube so go check them out and soak up some Eastern wisdom from an English gentleman.

19
We're All in Sales, Kid

AM I THE ONLY one that thinks everyone should work retail at least once in their life? How about restaurant work? Oh door to door sales, that's a toughy! I did door-to-door sales for about 5 months and was one of the most challenging jobs I ever had[13].

And why would I recommend such hardships? The challenges that came with the job made the experience invaluable. Your income was solely based on whether you could convince someone that just walked through their door to buy something from a stranger. And if you could do that, you could sell anything.

These jobs, which at first glance may seem unimportant and they don't pay very well. True, but they do give you a worthy skill, sales. I know what your thinking, I'm not a salesperson, I'm an artist. Well, guess what, you might be an artist, but you're also in sales, kid.

Whenever I go to an art festival, I see plenty of artists that flunk the basic sales 101 rules[14]. So here's a mythbuster for you: You are responsible for bringing value to your art. Your art DOES NOT sell itself.

So next time someone approaches your booth, here's a tip. Get off your phone, smile, be cheerful upbeat, and greet the person for God's sake. People will not buy from people they don't like, are annoyed with or are simply ignored by the artist. I know I certainly wouldn't. Think about it, it literally pays to be nice, especially in our field.

---

13 And I worked as a janitor, in an Alaskan cannery, a farm and a wood shop!
14 What the hell are they teaching you in that college of yours??

20

The Kaizen Method

Hey, do you remember newspapers? No? Well just go along with me. In a newspaper, there was a small insignificant section called, "On This Day[15]". In this section, they would list random facts about the day you were presiding. 'On this day, Lewis and Clark finally saw the sunset over the Pacific, On this Day, the first Shopping Cart was invented, On this Day, a tube of toothpaste was given a mint flavor.' You get it. They may seem like trivial facts but it made the random day you were in more significant in small ways. And this is how I decided to awkwardly segway to what is known as the Kaizen Method.

If you know it then congratulations. You're dismissed from class. If not, stay with me on this. The Kaizen method is a Japanese concept to mean daily improvement. It was developed after World War II to help improve efficiency. Understanding that significant change takes time and people don't like a radical change, the Kaizen method embraces small but frequent changes over longer periods of time. This method creates the least amount of effort but is also responsible for monumental progress. It's based on the idea that you can use daily improvements, no matter how small, for long-term change and growth. Slow and steady, my friend.

I like to take the Kaizen philosophy and adhere it to my personal life. Ask yourself, what did I learn today? If I have goals, did I move towards them, even if it was just a little bit? Keep track of your momentum.

> *"Excellence/Perfection is not a destination; it is a continuous journey that never ends."* — Brian Tracy

---

15 *For my hometown, it was on the second page in the lower right hand corner.*

21
What's Phubbing?

PHUBBING. SO THIS is a thing now and unfortunately, it's all too common.

Phubbing is when you pay more attention to your phone rather than the person that's in front of you. The word "phubbing" literally means phone snubbing. And the only reason why I know this is because it was being done to me consistently. Because it was so common[16], I didn't pay much attention to it but honestly, it was getting on my nerves. After having plenty of, "is it me?" thoughts, I did a little research. And come to find out, it isn't just me that's annoyed with their rude company.

Here's a reminder. The best thing you can do with the company you are keeping is to be present. That's it. Just be present and don't take them for granted. Outwardly snubbing aka "phubbing" the person in front of you will ultimately do serious damage to that relationship.

I ultimately think phones are doing damage, not just to our manners but to how our brains are adapting to constant stimuli. Sure, I just might be finally having my "old man shakes fist at clouds" moment and there's not much I can really do about it besides complain. But seriously, I challenge you to become your own lab rat in your very own psychological experiment. Put your phone down for a day and monitor your thoughts and feelings. And keep in mind that it wasn't long ago when we didn't walk around with these things.

---

16 Common doesn't equate to healthy but because it is so common, people have a tendency to put up with it, no matter how rude and annoying it is.

The Illusion of Multitasking

Many of us like to think we are great at multitasking. I'm sure you have seen that term in many job descriptions. You might have even claimed it as one of your strengths in your job interview.

I'm not sure why we make this a prerequisite for future employees. Perhaps because of its appearance. Assuming that we are all very busy equates to an illusion of productivity.

Here's the real deal on multitasking. Neuroscience will tell you that we don't simultaneously do two tasks at once. We toggle between them.

And no matter how busy we are, our brains are starting and stopping tasks. All this constant toggling between tasks makes us incredibly inefficient.

To do one thing well, you have to focus on, well, one thing. Cal Newport, author of "Deep Work" says we should move away from multitasking and start doing the opposite. We should start training our brains to focus on one thing for an extended period of time. In this day and age of distraction, that might be a challenge but it's a skill worth strengthening.

Deep Dive:
The Myth of Multitasking
https://www.psychologytoday.com/us/blog/creativity-without-borders/201405/the-myth-multitasking

23
Fight for your Right to Concentrate

We live in a distracting world. And since the advent of social media, which are well designed distracting machines, our brains have adapted. This might seem fine since humans are very adaptable creatures, but it's not serving us in this case. Social media has trained us to expect distraction, and if we are not constantly distracted, well then it must mean we're bored.

Again, in Cal Newport's book, "Deep Work," he makes a solid argument that we need to resist the urge of becoming constantly distracted. With all these distractions, we have fallen out of practice on being able to concentrate for long periods of time. And that's super important if you want to learn new things.

"To remain valuable in our economy, therefore, you must master the art of quickly learning complicated things. This task requires deep work. If you don't cultivate this ability, you're likely to fall behind as technology advances."

— Cal Newport

24

Immediacy Does Not Equal Importance

OUR BRAINS HAVE a bias towards immediacy and rightfully so. It meant to keep us alive and keep us on alert since the world was a dangerous place. Today there's a lot less danger but we still have the same brain. We have substituted all of the triggers of danger with bells and whistles, pop-ups and what-knots being delivered by our technical devices.

Again, these gadgets were cleverly designed to distract. Viva la resistance! No matter how difficult, remember, just because something is immediate (a phone call, a text, an e-mail) doesn't mean it's important.

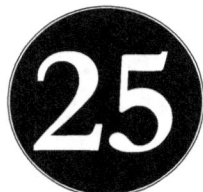

Learn How to Concentrate

Now that you know distractions aren't doing us any good, we really need to exercise our concentration muscles. There's a number of techniques, but my favorite is the "Pomodoro Technique"

Here's how it works:

1. Pick a task you need to concentrate on.
2. Get a timer. Any timer. Kitchen timers are perfect for this. Set the timer for 25 minutes.
3. Make a promise to yourself NOT to be distracted. No phones, computers, nada! For 25 minutes, you're going to do a concentration sprint.
4. When the buzzer goes off great! You did it and you reward yourself with a 5-minute break.
5. Repeat as many times as you need.

The reason why this technique is so successful is that it's a sprint of concentration. It's a short amount of time and you're rewarded with a short break at the end. Achievable short goals are easier to digest. And since there are easy (and will become easier since we are also strengthening our focus muscles), these Pomodoro sessions really do add up when it comes to productivity.

The reason why it's called a Pomodoro Technique is that before digital timers, you had the ol' fashion kitchen timers you set by hand, usually in the shape of a tomato. Pomodoro is Italian for 'tomato.'

26
Learn to Eat Frogs

LET'S FACE IT, eating frogs is a disgusting thought and Brian Tracy, the author of "Eat that Frog!" agrees. The main takeaway on this idea? Identify what's most important and what's your top goals. Once we identify them, make them a priority and do them first.

Simple right? We're pretty clever in our procrastination tactics. Busy work is a clever disguise for not doing that one thing that needs to be done. Especially when that one thing is difficult like eating a frog. And as we all know we love distractions, especially when it keeps us from eating a disgusting frog.

Use your primary time to tackle the actual things that matter the most. It may be an illusion especially when you're young, that we have an infinite amount of time. The sobering reality is that time is a finite resource. Work with a sense of urgency.

Deep Dive:
"Eat That Frog!" by Brian Tracy

27
Shiny Objects

As I've said, distractions come in many forms, especially when things get difficult. Anything worth doing has some level of difficulty. If it didn't, we would be bored with them. So when something gets to be a challenge, hang in their kitty and resist the temptation of finding other projects, greener grass, and projects that appear more attractive.

Here's an example. EVERYONE hates their job when they start. And why shouldn't they? They have no idea what's going on and you feel foolish while everyone looks like their masters at what they do. Here's the thing. Give yourself 3 months to hate your job. Three months. If by any chance you hate this job equally by the end of three months, then maybe the job really isn't a good fit and you should allow yourself to quit. What typically will happen is that you will find that you have gotten better, developed a passion for what you do, and have developed bonds with your coworkers.

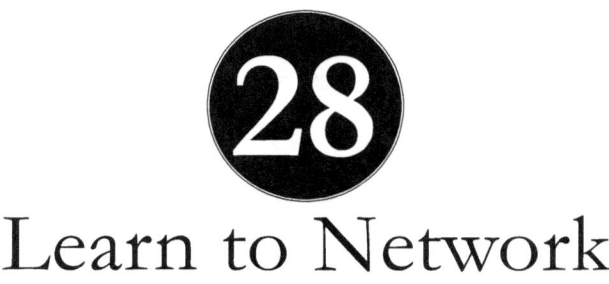

Learn to Network

Do you know a friend that only comes around when they need a favor? I'm sure you do. We all do. Don't be that person.

Networking is so important but it's also underestimated. Look for opportunities to build connections and to serve your community, your neighbors, friends, and family. And when there will be a time you will need a helping hand[17], helping hands will be there for you. It's the wonderful part of being and participating in a healthy community.

As the saying goes, "Don't build the well when you're thirsty."

Deep Dive:
    Jordan Harbinger's 6 minute Networking
    https://courses.jordanharbinger.com/courses/6-minute-networking

---

17 And trust me you'll probably will.

29

Surround Yourself with Smart People

YOU ARE THE AVERAGE of the people you spend the most time with so pick wisely. If you want to get good at any particular subject, get to know and spend time with the people that are already good at that subject. Simple enough. Now go out and find those people!

This is the basis of what is known as the Mastermind Principle and is what Napoleon Hill wrote in his book called, "Think and Grow Rich." The book, which is now a classic in the personal development niche, focuses on the many interviews Hill had with Andrew Carnegie. These talks with Carnegie which Hill saw as a mentor, ultimately changed Hill's life.

It's not important that you have all the knowledge and wisdom but rather that you have easy access to that knowledge and wisdom. The mastermind principle[18] is a simple yet powerful way of consolidating individual talents and abilities. A mastermind group is a group of your peers aligned together to help each member with their goals and problems. It's similar to the mentoring system but instead of having just one mentor, you have a group!

You don't have to persuade someone to mentor you. In today's world, we don't need these formalities. Just pick the surroundings and the people you admire and you can let it all happen by osmosis. You can even find groups online and you can't get anything more convenient than that.

---

18 Mastermind groups are still a common practice today but is only one principle out of many outlined in the book. This book was written in 1937 but is still read and studied today!

Deep Dive:
"Think and Grow Rich" by Napoleon Hill

30
Feature Creep

IF YOU HAVEN'T NOTICED, we humans have a bias towards more. The more the better seems to be America's modus operandi. And this concept goes way beyond consumerism too. Just take a look at your TV remote. Do you use all those functions? I would bet some serious money that you only use 20 percent of your remotes' buttons and those important functions can be hard to find. If it's true that we only use 20 percent of the functions on a remote, then why in hell are there so many freakin buttons? This is known as feature creep and it plagues all aspects of design.

It exists simply because it's much easier to add something than to take something away. And features tend to accumulate over time. Think of this case scenario. You have a team meeting of designers and engineers and other people with fancy degrees and titles. Your mission, to create a new fancy expensive remote control for a new fancy type expensive television. Thus, the brainstorming session begins. Unfortunately, Todd, the most annoyingly extroverted member of the team, already mentioned all the obvious buttons the remote should have: an on/off button in red, an up and down channel button, volume, numbers, all the obvious ones. Some team members now get a little antsy. They need to validate their positions at the table and put in our two cents. One mentions a Netflix button, another says we need an Amazon Prime button, and while we're at it a Hulu button as well. Now the buttons you had in mind have been spoken for and you want to add to the list too after feeling a little left out. "What about a dimming button and a blue light blocking button?" you say. Now Todd, Mr. on/off button guy, isn't going to be outdone by some measly dimming switch idea. "Oh!" He blurts out. "We need buttons to toggle between devices! And maybe we can control those devices with their own set of buttons!" And it goes on and on...

Now your team should be allowed to mention anything and everything in a brainstorming session. That's divergent thinking for you[19]. But that doesn't mean all suggestions ought to make the cut. But in many cases they do. Why? As you saw in my silly example, it's office politics. But besides that, our bias towards "more is always better" kicks in. We tell ourselves, why not? Lots of buttons make it more valuable. But unfortunately, this kind of feature creep can be expensive and even make the product overly complicated.

When your designing, adding components is only natural. But understanding our own natural bias to 'more' means that the other half of the design process is to clean up, subtract and simplify.

---

19 We'll get to what exactly that is.

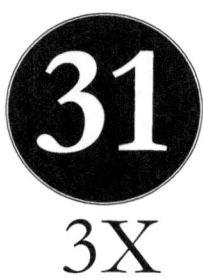

3X

HERE'S A VALUABLE LESSON I learned years ago. I was introduced to a wealthy, older and quite an eccentric couple that wanted a mural painted in their New England colonial home[20]. I was just starting as an artist and although I had some painting experience, I've never painted on someone's wall. I wasn't a muralist just yet, but I was confident that if I broke the project down step by step, I could figure it out. It was a challenge, but I always liked challenges.

The person that introduced me was my friend Bert, master carpenter[21]. He was replacing a few windows and mentioned my name. Thankfully he bigged me up by telling them I was a talented upcoming artist. No pressure right?

The first interview went well and they like my sketches. Then came the part of the conversation all beginning artists dread to talk about. Price. I chickened out and told them I would get back to them on that.

Later I met Bert and he asked me how it went.
"Well. They want me to paint the mural."
"Great! So how much are you going to charge them?"
Figuring out how the square footage of the wall, I was proud that I used some logic in coming up with a price. I told him the amount I came up with.
Bert just nodded as he expected to hear some nonsense answer from a rookie.
"OK that's good, but do yourself a favor...."
"Yeah what's that?" I said.

---

20 Newport, RI has the most concentrated 18th century housing in the country. It really is like going back to a different time!
21 The same mentor who showed me how to lathe a baseball bat.

"Take that number you just gave me and multiply it by three."

It was a number that made me uncomfortable but since he was speaking from experience, I knew he was probably right. We tend to overestimate what we can do in a given amount of time. I went back and gave them my estimate. Although they were taken back by the amount, they ultimately agreed.

As Bert's prediction rang true, it took a lot longer than I first estimated. And thankfully, they were happy with the results.

The moral of the story: don't be afraid to ask for top dollar. This brings us to the next obstacle beginning artists always face...

32
Free Exposure

THIS ONE IS LAUGHABLE because I have no idea why this is exclusive for creative types. You wouldn't ask a plumber to fix your leaks for free exposure or a farmer to give you free produce so that you could tell your neighbors how great their carrots are!

Listen up all creative type people! You musicians, crafters, artisans, and artists of all types, remember one thing; if you're giving something of value, you ought to expect something of value in return[22]. It should be a "win-win" situation and I'm here to tell you, don't fall for the oldest trick in the book called, "free exposure." Because the only advertising you're going to get in return is that your the creative person that does good work for free.

Please don't confuse this with doing pro bono work. If you're an established artist and want to give back to a worthy cause, that's awesome. Go for it! But call it for what it is and be careful and selective to what you say yes to.

---

22 And this means that it doesn't always have to be money. It's just a value-for-value kind of thang. I've worked on farms for produce, which I was going to buy from them anyway so it all worked out.

33
Learning To Say NO

YOU HAVE EVERY RIGHT to say no to anything. You also have the right not to give a reason why you said no in the first place. This is a lesson it seems you don't learn until later in life but it's a good one to get a head start on.

When you're young, you're ambitious. You're full of energy and more apt to take on more than what you can chew. You're also more apt to give a tentative yes, although you wished you had the kahunas to say no[23].

If you don't want to do something, just say no. It's your obligation, not just to yourself, but to the person that might have wanted to do that project.

---

23 Trust me, I've been here many times and learned this lesson many times, the hard way.

34

Be the Right Candidate

I THOUGHT ABOUT this during a job interview. It's not enough to just have the right skills. If it was up to me, skill sets would be secondary. Having the right mindset - that is, the willingness to learn, grow, listen, ask questions, be humble and positive - is far more important than finding an employee with an exact list of skills. In my opinion, the right people can learn, develop and thrive under the right work culture.

Imagine you were a manager of a sports team. Yay sports ball! There's always a temptation to spend the money to get a superstar. Although these superstars are obviously great players, they hardly make great team players. Superstars might get you a little success in the short term but solid teams, teams with players who are willing to learn together, cooperate and collaborate, win championships.

I have heard employers say, 'it's hard to find good workers' in which I reply, 'yes, but it's also hard to find good employers.'

35 Interview the Interviewer

I THINK WE FORGET or perhaps we don't know, that an interview goes both ways. So if you feel intimidated in an interview for a job, flip it around and interview them. We might have assumed it's suppose to be one-sided, where all the power is on the side of the employer. Oh, Contrare!

Research the company and ask them questions. Lots of questions. Keep in mind that you want to know if this position and company is a good match for you, not just you for them.

Here are a few of my favorite questions you might think about asking:
- What are the biggest challenges that someone in this position would face?
- What does a typical day look like?
- What are the skills and experiences you're looking for in an ideal candidate?
- What is the company's culture like?
- What attributes would I need to be successful in this role?
- What training programs are available to your employees?
- Are there opportunities for professional development?
- What are your expectations of this position over the next 6 - 12 months?
- What's your favorite part about working here?
- Can you tell me about the company's future? How does it plan to grow?
- Who will I work with most closely?
- Is there anything else I can provide you with that would be helpful?

Deep Dive:
    For a full list of questions, check out this blog post:
    https://www.themuse.com/advice/51-interview-questions-you-should-be-asking

36

How You Do One Thing...

...IS HOW YOU DO EVERYTHING. Really? Let's put it this way, how someone behaves, even in small inconspicuous ways, leaves clues about that person's mindset, personality, and morals[24].

And this certainly goes for businesses. Recently I had a job interview for a graphic design position for a good size corporation. The first interview went well and they called me for a second interview. They stood me up on the second interview[25] and without an apology, reached out to reschedule. While I was waiting for the second interview to begin (again), they called me and canceled saying they have just filled the position. Sigh. The next week I get another call from the same company saying they would like to finally give me that second interview as the candidate they picked didn't work out. "No thank you." was my reply. And this rule goes for ourselves...

If you're going to do a job, whether that's painting the Sistine Chapel, sweeping the floor at a supermarket, or interviewing a potential employee, do them all equally well. Approach any project, big or small with this idea: everything and anything you do will have your signature on it.

---

24 For anyone that's still dating, pay attention to how your date treats the wait staff at a restaurant. If your date is treating people rudely, simply because they feel they can get away with it, run!
25 These are digital zoom interviews and from my recent experience, employers are not treating them with the same amount of gravitas as an in-person interview.

37

Macs are Useless in the Corporate World

AND THIS IS COMING from a Mac lover! Well, they're not completely useless, I was just trying to get a rise out of you. But they are a pain in the ass when it comes to the everyday corporate PC world. I'll explain...

A few years ago, I landed a job with a corporation. Before my first day, my new boss asked, "so what do you want to work on, a mac or a PC?"

'Ooooh, I had a choice! How luxurious!' I thought. During my Peace Corps [26] service, I brought a mac with me but it broke one year into my service and was desperate to get something fast and cheap. So of course I got a much cheaper PC[27].

"I'll take a mac!" These are words I regretted for the year I was with the company. By the way, the mac worked fine but that wasn't the problem. The problem was that the mac, being the only one in the office I later found out, didn't play nicely with the rest of the technical PC-based system the company was using. It was quite the challenge for our IT person[28]. Fortunately for me, they gave me a backup PC to fill in the gaps when my mac just didn't cut it. Just simply printing or connecting to an online meeting was a major chore with a mac. With a PC? No problem at all.

Lesson: Macs are great but can be a hassle within a dominant PC

---

26 Not that long ago I dropped out, abandoned graphic design, and went into the Peace Corps.
27 I ended up liking PCs surprisingly enough and continue to work on them today. Sorry, Apple.
28 Especially with organizations where privacy and security is super duper important. And God bless the IT person at my last job because I gave her quite a technical workout!

environment. If I could do it all over, I would have answered my future boss's question with a question. "What does everyone else have?" Also, it pays off to be able to work comfortably on both systems.

38
Tailor Your Resume

I KNOW THIS IS A PAIN, especially in the age where most potential employers don't feel they need to get back to you after you painstakingly entered all your information on their website. It's a pain but it also pays off. Here's a tip:

Copy the job description text from a job board and paste it into an online cloud generator. There's more than a few online. Now take a look at what comes up. The larger words you see in the word cloud are the ones that were mentioned more frequently, so there's a safe assumption that those words are uber important. Find a way to work these words into your resume.

39

The Briefcase Method

THANKFULLY, BECAUSE OF your tailored resume, you finally got an interview. Great! You made it through the first phase of the filtering process and now entering round two. Your new challenge is to stand out, from the now smaller crowd, because you're definitely not the only one being interviewed that week. Here's how you do that.

Now you don't necessarily need a briefcase although that would be nice. The briefcase technique, in short, means you're bringing something of value to the table, literally. Study up on the company, and do some market research. Hit them with some ideas, recommendations, research, and print them out. These sheets can be a nice addition to your interview because you want to make the impression you're willing to go above and beyond to serve the cause. In addition, there's something to be said about offering something tangible like a nicely designed printed piece. Sending the same information virtually just doesn't have the same perceived value.

Deep Dive:
The Briefcase Technique by Ramit Sethi
https://www.youtube.com/watch?v=NViqHCrljf8

40
Jobs are the Riskiest Investments

So now that you are employment with a great job and a promising future, please allow me to ruin that for you.

I recently browsed Indeed.com and found a graphic design job listing. There were plenty of design job posts but this one caught my attention. In the description was a litany of requirements, a long list of responsibilities with at least 5 years of design experience. Going rate? Fifteen bucks an hour. Really? Are these companies delusional? Isn't that going to be the minimum wage for the US within a few years?

So out of curiosity, I went to their website. I played a video explaining the company and its corporate culture. The CEO then made the unfortunate claim… "When you come to work for us, you're family." Oh realllllly? I have heard this one before, and I'll have to apologize for upfront for my salty mindset when I say this but, DON'T BELIEVE THEM! YOU ARE NOT FAMILY!

Would a family fire another family member from the family? Would your son, daughter, wife, mom, husband cease being your family because the numbers in Q4 were lower than expected? Sorry son, I took a look at the numbers and it looks like it's just not working out. Not bloody likely.

Calling an employee a family member is just plain wrong. Calling them a team member, however, is probably more accurate. Teams work and cooperate together and it's about performance. Being a part of a team means you bring value to the table. Hopefully, the value is an even exchange.

So there's no unconditional family love going on in a company. Sure they could love love love you one day and literally lay you off the next. I've seen this happen. It happened to me and it has happened to plenty of hard-working employees. That's why jobs are the riskiest investment you could ever make.

What to do? Build and buy assets that will eventually create passive income[29]. Work on your side hustles and develop multiple streams of income. Easier said than done right? Sure it's a challenge but so is today's job market.

Deep Dive:
"**Rich Dad, Poor Dad**" **by Robert Kiyosaki**
www.richdad.com

---

29 Here's a caveat. It's best to stay away from any 'get rich schemes' and pretty much all multi-level marketing companies. The lure for easy passive money is great but resist the urge. There's no such thing as easy and passive. All the passive money I have earned took a great amount of effort, it's just that you are putting the effort upfront.

Your Job is your Patron

ARTISTS THROUGHOUT THE centuries have always relied on rich benefactors. I was lucky to have one of these rich benefactors who paid me well to paint murals.

So you don't happen to have your own personal Medici? Think of your job as your patron. How so? It's a matter of mindset[30].

Don't think of your job as an obstacle but as a vehicle that allows you to do your art on your off time. It supports your studio/apartment, pays whatever bills you have and all of your art supplies. Why am I trying to force a positive spin on what could be a shitty job situation for some people? Well, reframing your shitty job situation makes it easier to do something you don't like doing, like said shitty jobs. How? Because it's a necessary means to an end and your ends are worth it.

---

30 *And mindset is everything.*

Clients not Customers

You may think they are the same but there's a difference. A major difference. Let's take a look at the differences...

Customers are:
- An exchange of a good or service for money
- Buy either for price and/or value

Clients are:
- Buy because they trust you and your brand
- Have a long term relationship with you and your company

What are our mindsets when it comes to customers vs clients?

We treat Customers like:
- Looking to extract money from
- Customers come and go
- Shallow relationship

We treat Clients like:
- We're looking to help solve their problems
- We're looking to serve
- We're looking to create a long term relationship

It's not that customer relationships should always be considered a bad thing but, if we are in the art business, we need to develop relationships with clients. And if we treat them as clients, we don't look at them as paydays but rather someone we are in service to, solving a problem they are willing to trust us with.

43

Find Beauty in the Ordinary

A VERY LONG TIME AGO, I had this crazy notion that photography was easy. My thought behind that was, 'all you have to do is push a button, and voila! Instant art! What's the big deal right?' That was right up until I took a photography class[31].

Not so fast little grasshopper. Capturing ordinary life is easy but here lies the challenge: As an artist, it's our job to find the extraordinary within the ordinary. We could even show a new perspective on the ordinary that could reveal its inner "extraordinary-ness."

What is common may be seen as ordinary, we've seen it a million times and we simply take it for granted. This challenge of seeing the beauty and the interesting all around us is not just for the photographers. It's advice for any artist that might be searching for the interesting when it's right in front of us.

My advice is to not take the slightest details for granted. You just might find extraordinary beauty in the most benign, overlooked objects of everyday life. If you're not convinced, take a look at a brilliant Czech animator and filmmaker, Jan Švankmajer.

---

31 *My apologies photographers. In my defense, I was young and naive. And now I'm just naive.*

The Good, the Bad, and the Ugly in Design

As an artist, you have a keen eye for details. And I'm sure you have experienced the good and bad in design. If you haven't noticed, it's everywhere and I'm not just talking about websites and posters. Design is literally everything and everywhere.

Signs, packages, tables, doors, your TV remote, my 2002 Toyota Echo, etc. all of it was designed by persons and they were designed (hopefully) with a human in mind.

I took a hilarious stab at product design once. My grandmother, who had cable, only wanted to watch one channel. All she cared about was ME TV that showed reruns of old sitcoms (Three's Company I believe was her favorite). Now my grandmother, who couldn't see very well, in addition to being very tech-challenged, had a hard time finding the station. The call number for the channel was 27. That's when I came up with what I thought was a perfect solution. I bought a remote, programmed it for your TV, and took all the buttons off except the 2 and the 7 and of course, the on/off button and volume. Problem solved, right? A week later I called to see how she was making out with her beautifully designed remote.

"Terrible! It doesn't work," she said.
"Terrible? Why terrible?" I was surprised by her answer.
"Well I tried your remote but the only channel I can get is 72."

As artists, it's not only our job to point out what's good or bad or ugly. We have to know why they are good or bad or ugly. The world is full of all three. Critique the designs you experience in the world, speak the language of design, and stay in practice. Just from this simple practice of observation will ultimately make you a better artist and designer.

When People Zig, Zag

THE CROWDS ARE NOT always correct. Strike that. They are rarely correct. Crowd behavior can be based on not well thought out ideas, irrationality, strong emotions, and tribal thinking. Group thought can lead us down dangerous paths like lemmings going off a cliff.

Rather than following the herd, learn how to develop what's known as an informed opinion. It might not be a popular opinion, but don't go for popular when you're going for the objective truth.

Being irrational creatures, we can get emotionally invested in our opinions. And social media is notorious for feeding the ideas we agree with, further solidifying our confirmation bias. In the age of partisanship, we have developed a hypersensitive hysteria to opposing ideas. So that's the zig part, now let me tell you more about the zag.

An Informed Opinion

In the ecosystem of thought, an informed opinion is on the top of the food chain. This is because it's an opinion as a result of researching both sides of an argument without judgment. This takes time and effort, not to mention a considerable amount of emotional constraint, which is probably why most people don't have to carry them. But if you're willing to put in the time, you will not only have a better understanding of your own opinion but your opponent's position as well[32].

---

32 Not to say that people with opposing opinions are your opponent. I have plenty of friends and relatives with numerous opposing ideas and I have stopped a long time ago trying to convince them of mine. Trust me, the effort of trying to change other people's minds will be futile and unappreciated.

You can write a whole book on how to develop an intelligent opinion. I'm not going to do that. But hopefully, I can set you off on the right path. Below is a link to designer and CEO extraordinaire Chris Do. This is a useful workshop on how to work towards becoming a master within any given field. And luckily for us, it doesn't take 10,000 hours.

Deep Dive:

Chris Do from the Futur has a solution in developing a path to mastery or at least get very close to it. Here it is:

- Read 5 books on the same subject, the subject you want to have an informed opinion on.
- Review and compare these books, ask questions and find multiple answers to those questions.
- Form your own opinion. A now informed opinion.

Time is on Your Side when it Comes to This

...AND THIS IS THE MAGIC of compounding interest.

> *"The magic of compounding interest is truly the eighth wonder of the world."*
> — Albert Einstein

If you don't know this rule, well it's about time you did. It's called "The Rule of 72" and here's how it works:

Interest Rate/ 72 = Time required to double an investment

Easy Peasy! For example, if you had a bizarre high return of interest at 36% (wouldn't that be nice) you would double your investment in only 2 years! Seventy-two years divided by thirty-six. Wahoo! What about a more realistic 5% return? Just a little over 14 years.

If you're young - and I'm thinking you are - you have time on your side and that's a very very good thing. Don't make the mistake most people make and take care of their retirement when it's close to retiring. That's bananas. Don't be bananas.

It's OK to Ask For Help

THE SINGLE MISTAKE people make early on is that they try to do it "all" on their own. The truth is that many, if not all successful people, have been mentored, coached, or just found the right company to keep. Perhaps being American has done this to us. It's deep within our cultural narrative to try to raise ourselves up from our bootstraps[33]. Blame it all on the idea of rugged individualism. It's tempting to try to do it all yourself but remember this, success doesn't happen in a vacuum. So feel free to ask for help, get a coach or a teacher and if your lucky enough, get a few mentors for good measure.

---

33 As you already know, this isn't possible.

48

One Reason Why You Should Teach Someone

If you really want to learn something, teach it. Let's take a quick look at what's called, "The Feynman Technique." The technique is simple. If you have a subject matter that you assume you know up and down and sideways, put yourself to the test. Explain it to someone that's not an expert in the field. Because according to Feynman, there's a big difference between understanding the subject and knowing the subject. The Illusion of Mastery bias is convincing yourself that you have mastered the subject simply because you understood the subject when the subject was being explained.

Force yourself to articulate what you have learned and notice any shortcomings or gaps. If there are any, you're now aware of your weak spots and what you need to improve on.

> *"The person who says he knows what he thinks but cannot express it usually does not know what he thinks."*
> — Mortimer Adler

Reference:
Richard Feynman
https://fs.blog/2012/04/feynman-technique/

Learn to Take an Existential Punch

OUR PROFESSIONS, NO MATTER how attached we are to them, is not who we are. And perhaps this is easier for, let's say an accountant to recognize than us artists. Artists are so entrenched in their work, it might be difficult to separate the art from the artist. But it's well worth reminding ourselves of our attachments, whether that's our profession, our thoughts, opinions, beliefs, what have you, and the angst we may experience when we imagine ourselves letting go.

If you then ask the question, 'well if I'm not that, then what am I?" Ah, welcome to existentialism 101! And you don't have to agree with it or like it but please entertain this thought just for a minute. Perhaps life is much much larger than our careers, jobs, our thoughts and emotions, and all of the myopic views and self-identities we became very comfortable in.

Now, let's go back to us as artists and our close attachments to our creations. These attachments may seem non-existent but as soon as we get some feedback on our creations and that feedback comes in the form of criticism, we're tempted to initially feel anger and may even take it as a personal attack.

This is why it's a benefit to detach ourselves from the end product and to remember, we are not what we do[34]. When we come to this conclusion, it's much easier to not take criticism[35] personally. Besides that, the feedback might be very helpful. If it's not, then don't take the advice. It's that simple.

---

34 I get it, you don't agree. I sometimes don't agree. That's how strong these attachments are.
35 With the assumption that the criticism is in the form of positive criticism.

50

But Don't Be a Punching Bag

Despite what I've said on the previous page, it doesn't mean you should be taking punches that are actually trying to do you harm. So if you feel[36] people are crossing the line, then call them out on it.

Not being a punching bag is not to be confused with being hypersensitive or being defensive. It means having enough respect for yourself and that you're worth defending and willing to defend the healthy boundaries you've created to protect yourself[37].

---

36 And it's definitely a feel.
37 It took me a while to finally develop well-defined boundaries with people. Interestingly enough, when these boundaries are enforced, the "toxic" simply dissipate from your life.

51
Within Structure Thrives Creativity

WERE YOU EVER given a project where the teacher told you could do whatever you wanted? You get to choose the subject matter, the medium, it was all up to you. Whatever your heart desired. At first glance, this sounded like a dream project. But did you struggle to start it? I would be very surprised to hear no. And that's why art projects are not these free-for-all assignments.

Creativity, in a paradoxical way, thrives when it's contained within a structure. Our brains are problem-solving machines. But it needs to know what the challenges are before we start coming up with the solutions. So to jump-start your creativity, create a set of rules for yourself. Within these perimeters, you'll be surprised just how creative you can be.

52
Look to Serve

To get, you have to give. This is a universal law. And to be happy, truly happy, we have to stop focusing so much on ourselves and start focusing on others. In a way, serving others is a great remedy for our own blues.

Robert Allen wrote a book called, "The Four Maps Of Happy Successful People." In the book, he explains that there are three reasons that motivate us, *Need Reasons, Me Reasons,* and *We Reasons*. The need reasons are self-explanatory, it's what we need to sustain ourselves. Once those are taken care of, we move to the Me reasons and that's the common, 'I want a million dollars, I want to be pretty, I want, I want I want,' etc. Those reasons are definitely driving, motivating forces, but once we get there, we are always left empty. That brings us to the We Reasons. Our We Reasons is the motivation for helping others, our communities, and focusing our endeavors outward. As we get older, we realize that these are the real reasons for getting out of bed in the morning. We reasons are incredibly powerful drivers and can also be the main suppliers of happiness and purpose.

Deep Dive:
 "The Four Maps Of Happy Successful People" by Robert Allen

53

Don't Fake It Til' You Make It. Do This Instead

When you are starting off, how do we establish credibility? Many of us use the infamous advice, "Fake it to you make it."

According to Chris Do, founder of the design agency, "The Futur," there's a word in that advise phrase that can easily trip us up. That word is "fake."

None of us want to be associated with the word fake, so why are we using this as a positive affirmation? Chris Do advises us to stop using this phrase and try this instead:

"Believe it until you Achieve it."

This might come across as a bit "meta" but I don't care because I lean into the "meta" at times. Your imagination is the seed to reality. When you believe that it's possible, then you're opening up the possibilities of achieving it. Everything that was invented, that we you use on a daily basis and probably take for granted, was at one time only a an idea.

Deep Dive:
  "Fake It Till You Make It Explained" by Chris Do, The Futur
  https://www.youtube.com/watch?v=vHlLtOzSjks

54

Passive Income as an Artist

THERE'S NEVER BEEN a better time for making passive income as a creative person. A simple Google search will give you many avenues to explore, from producing stock photography, video and audio footage, making your own fonts, patterns, crafts, stickers to publishing how-to books, teaching courses and tutorials, etc. I mean there's a lot.

The possibilities are endless. Will this get you rich? Probably not[38]. It's more of a get-rich sloooww scheme. It's the strategy of building slow, steady, and multiple streams of revenue while you are busy working on your main gig. And if those revenue streams one day match the revenue of your 9 to 5, well then work becomes optional. And that's a great position to be in.

---

38 Although there have been many artists that have turned selling their art online as a full-time gig!

55

Time is Money but Money is NEVER Time

HERE'S A SHORT EXCERPT from Seneca's book, On the Shortness of Time:

"It is not that we have a short space of time, but that we waste much of it. Life is long enough, and it has been given in sufficiently generous measure to allow the accomplishment of the very greatest things if the whole of it is well invested. But when it is squandered in luxury and carelessness, when it is devoted to no good end, forced at last by the ultimate necessity we perceive that it has passed away before we were aware that it was passing. So it is—the life we receive is not short, but we make it so, nor do we have any lack of it, but are wasteful of it."

I would never advocate for people to be stingy. In fact, I think people should be generous whenever possible. But there's one thing we all have the right to be stingy with and that's our time. Time is a finite resource and unlike money, if you run out, you can't make more of it.

Don't take time for granted. Make everyday count.

Deep Dive:
  "On the Shortness of Life" by Seneca

Find Time

SPEAKING OF TIME, it may seem that we never have enough. But as Seneca taught us, life is long enough, it's how we live our lives and spend our time that's the problem.

Let's use Scott Adams, the creator of the cartoon strip Dilbert as an example. He wasn't always an artist. In fact, his whole comic strip is based on his cubicle corporate experience. Since his job took most of his prime time, he decided to wake up 2 hours earlier to practice his drawing. He decided to give himself his own prime time, the beginning of the day when he felt the freshest to improve on his own craft[39]. Now that's dedication!

There's always time for the thing you passionately want to do. You just need to make room for it.

Deep Dive:
  "How to Fail at Almost Everything and Still Win Big: Kind of the Story of My Life" by Scott Adams

---

39 Most people feel the "freshest" or the most clear-headed in the morning but we all know that's not everyone. You might be one of those weird night owls. I'm, however with Scott on this one and rather leave the night for resting.

57

Embrace the Present Moment

"There's no time like the present."

Although the quote should read, "There's no other time than the present." The present moment is the moment we will always be in. The future and the past is just an abstraction.

Like Eckart Tolle gives us in his now infamous book, "The Power of Now,

"The Past fills us with regret. ...
The Future fills us with anxiety. ...
The Present is the only time we have control. ..."

58

Why you Should Learn Marketing

As artists, we have inherited the belief that our work should speak for itself. This is false. Your work is probably good but that's not good enough. Why? Because a), you need to find your audience aka tribe and b), you need to convince your audience that your product is the right product for them. Easier said than done but this is why we should shed this "art speaks for itself" notion and with it our pretentious attitude that sales and marketing are below us.

If you want to start with a solid foundation in marketing, you don't have to go any further than Seth Godin. Seth has been leading the charge on what marketing really is and how we should do it and how we should not.

Here's what marketing is in a nutshell and why you shouldn't be afraid of it. Good marketing, to its very basic core, is the simple art of persuasion. It is not scamming or hustling people out of their money. It is not pressuring someone to buy something they don't need or want. It is not hyping something, giving false promises, manipulation, or lying about your product. All that is bad bad bad marketing and it's given the industry a terrible stereotype.

Good marketing is knowing your customers. It's becoming empathetic to your tribe, understanding them, and showing up to be helpful. This marketing is about solving problems, your customers' problems. It's about being authentic, sincere, generous, and confident to share your story and what you made.

Yes, it's about influence but it's an influence that leads to improvement and change for the better. Good marketing allows them to be agents for changes that can improve their customer's lives, their communities, and ultimately the world.

> *"Marketers make things better by making change happen."*
> –Seth Godin

Deep Dive:
"This is Marketing" by Seth Godin

59
What is Brand

Many designers[40] get confused when they talk about brand. What actually is it? We might say it's a logo, the look and feel, the color palette, a slogan, etc. Hell, it's all in the style guide, right? Well, not really. Think of it this way, brand is what people say about the company when the company is not in the room. Brand is simply the company's personality.

It's what the market says it is and not what the company says it is. Confused? Please please please check out the example below by Marty Neumeier. He explains it perfectly and with pictures! Something this book is sadly missing.

Does brand matter? Just ask Apple and Coca-Cola. Much of their company's equity comes from their brand's reputation.

Deep Dive:
  "Zag" by Marty Neumeier
  www.martyneumeier.com/brand-illustrated

---

40 *When I say many, I really mean me.*

60
Why Reading is Not Enough

CALLING ALL GRAPHIC DESIGNERS! If you haven't heard the name Chris Do and the company he created called The Futur yet, do yourself a favor and get yourself acquainted. Chris drops a lot of value, and not just about design-ee stuff. A lot of it relates to self-improvement.

In this webinar (link below), Chris tells us that reading and consuming content isn't enough. Now I love to read and I love books. They're many books I have read that have inspired me but if I was to recall the takeaways a year later, it would be a struggle.

This is Chris's point. Passively absorbing content isn't enough. Here's what he suggests:

- After each chapter, review what you have learned.
- Write and take notes. What are the main points?
- Ask questions. Do you question any of the material? Compare it with another author on the same subject. This is your pathway to an informed opinion we learned about earlier.
- Act. Doing is the best way to learn. Put your newfound knowledge to use.
- Teach. Teaching someone helps solidify your learning and you get to learn your newfound knowledge twice[41].

Deep Dive:
    Chris Do, The Futur

---

41 This is the Feynman Technique in action.

61

Design With the Customer in Mind

THIS SOUNDS LIKE I'm overstating the obvious but sometimes we have to go back to the basics.

Whenever we are making, designing, producing, creating, as artists we tend to create it for ourselves. This is fine if you want to do art for art's sake. But if we want to sell and perhaps sell as much as possible, we need to focus on an audience, our audience, and what they want[42]. Is this what they call "selling out?" Sure. But when we're in the business of making something for someone else for the sake of profit, we're ALL selling out and that isn't necessarily a bad thing.

When designing it doesn't hurt to identify your ideal customer[43]. Take a look from their perspective. Step into their shoes. It will give you a fresh perspective and a needed break from your own.

---

42 Now hopefully what we create and what our audience is looking to buy line up but they don't always.
43 Oops sorry I mean client!

62
Sharing is Caring

DON'T FORGET TO show your work. Do you think artists need to be told that? Am I overstating the obvious again? Probably, but not according to Austin Kleon who wrote a whole book on it.

Here's what Austin has to say. Don't worry about being perfect. People don't relate to perfect anyway. Showing your work doesn't mean only showing the end project. People want to know your secret sauce!

Sharing is about generosity and generosity is infectious. Being secretive means you have bought into the zero-sum game[44]. That's another way of saying, 'there ain't enough to go around and you want your share.' By the way, that mindset sucks. The universe is an abundant resource. Sharing is not only helpful for others since we can all rise from your wisdom and unique perspective on the world, but people you connect with are more willing to be reciprocated. Be the change and act as a role model. That's how you're going to save the world.

Deep Dive:
"Show your Work!" by Austin Kleon

---

[44] *I've been around artists that have well guarded their secrets!*

63 Please Learn Typography

Hey, I got an idea! Do you want to stand out as a graphic designer? Learn Typography. Seriously. It seems like a dying skill and maybe we could blame it on the advent of desktop publishing. Typography is important to graphic design and shouldn't be neglected. Even the basics would put you miles ahead of your peers.

Ascender descender, baseline, cap line, tracking vs kerning, font vs typeface, widows, and rivers. Get to know these terms and impress your friends and teachers! Great for ice breakers at parties!

Deep Dive:
Want to build your kerning chops? Here's an app only a typographer nerd would love!
https://type.method.ac

The Starving Artist Myth

GREAT ARTISTS AREN'T the starving kind and starving doesn't make you a great artist. Some great artists have "starved" in the past but starving didn't make them great, it's just what they got.

Trivia question. How much money did Michelangelo have? Accounts have on record that he complained about money problems. Was he poor or just being a drama llama? Believe it or not, Michelangelo would have been worth 47 million dollars to today's standards. That's far from being a starving artist. But why is that so surprising? It's because it doesn't fit the story, the story we all were told that an artist willing to make their way in the world is just asking for a whole heap of trouble.

So please don't be a martyr. It doesn't serve you or anyone. Eat well, go to the gym, get a good night's sleep, and take care of your body, mind, soul, and of course, your finances. Then make art for God's sake!

> *"The greater danger for most of us lies not in setting our aim too high and falling short; but in setting our aim too low, and achieving our mark."*
> —Michelangelo Buonarotti

Deep Dive:
"Real Artists Don't Starve[45]" by Jeff Goins

---

[45] *Honestly, I haven't read this one...yet, but it looks like we all could read this book and smash this myth to pieces once and for all!*

65

The Attitude of Gratitude

IN ADDITION, WE should never take our abundance and wealth for granted. You can get a quick lesson in appreciation by living in an undeveloped or developing country. Washing your clothes in a 5-gallon bucket for 2 years will definitely make you appreciate a washing machine and dryer.

Practice gratitude. Always. Here's a little tip for those who suffer from bouts of insomnia. Before you go to sleep, recall your day and think of 5 things you're grateful for. This simple practice of gratitude, believe it or not, will help you sleep the whole night through.

66

Don't Vilify the Wealthy

THE WEALTHY AREN'T MORE greedy and they aren't any less virtuous than us. I have worked and painted murals for wealthy patrons. Although eccentric at times, I found them friendly, generous, warm, and appreciative.

Moral of the story. There is no link between our virtues and what's in our bank accounts. If we examine our relationship with money, we might find hangups and guilt our subconscious has been holding onto for years. These are worth seriously looking into because they could be the source of our self-sabotage, especially when it comes to our finances. Once you're aware, you then have control over building a new, healthy financial mindset and on the path to an optimal life.

Deep Dive:
"You Are a Badass at Making Money" by Jen Sincero

67
Effective is More Important than Pretty

FUNNY STORY. When I was shopping around for a job I got an interview with a small toy manufacturer. Proud of my portfolio (and yes, we actually had to carry big clunky black portfolio cases to interviews back then) containing real-life projects, I lugged my work to the interview. As my interviewer was flipping through the pages, I felt some good vibes. He seemed impressed and was getting some positive nods.

"These all look great," he said.
"Thank you."
"Unfortunately I can't use you."
"Oh, Okaaaaay."
He went on to explain. "You see, you're designs are all very well done. Very pleasing to the eye. Our packaging has to be loud, abstruse, on the verge of being obnoxious." I was confused but just politely nodded.

"Most of our products are positioned near the cashier line. So it's our goal to get the most attention as possible, especially with children who are too riled up not to take no for an answer. I'm afraid you would hate designing for us."

Um did I just fail an interview for having good work? I think I just did.

Design goes beyond just making something look gorgeous. Good design in the marketplace has objectives other than aesthetics. Communication is always number one and sometimes it's just getting bratty kids to bully their parents into buying them a crappy toy.

68

The Oppression of Choice

IT'S A PARADOX. We assume the more choice we have the better. But more choices cause us decision fatigue. And this is fatigue we like to avoid. Take the case of an experiment illustrated in Barry Schwartz's book, "The Paradox of Choice."

At a farmer's market, there are two sellers of jams and jellies. One has what would seem like an infinite amount of flavors. The other? Six. Now, if you stop and surveyed people which jam seller did you prefer, they would overwhelmingly say the one with the infinite amount of choices. But who sold more? The one with the six choices.

People may say that more choice is better but keep in mind that making decisions is exhausting. Adding more choices causes people to compare. More choice, more thinking we have to do[46].

Something to keep in mind when you're selling jellies or art. Don't overwhelm your client with too many choices and help them along in their decision-making.

Deep Dive:
"The Paradox of Choice" by Barry Schwartz

---

46 Maybe this is why most people hate food shopping?

The Psychology of Color

COLOR HAS POWER OVER US. Why shouldn't it, we evolved around the stuff and have a primordial relation with it. Allow me to tell one of my favorite examples to illustrate how powerful color is:

There was once a lake made from an abandoned quarry in Scotland. The lake was a beautiful cyan blue. Natural formations of calcium leach into the lake making the Ph of the water extremely alkaline. The lake was clear from any living thing including algae. Tourists who visited the lake fell under the lake's spell of its beautiful blue color. Many of them jumped in to take a dip.

Since the water of the lake has the same ph as bleach, these people got hurt. The village near the lake knew of the dangers of the lake and have peppered the area with signs describing its dangers and why the water is dangerous.

Despite the number of signs, people under the spell of its clear blue water continued to jump in and continued to get hurt.

The village was perplexed. The signs don't seem to work. Until one person had an idea[47]. Instead of putting up more signs which seem to be useless, the community was advised to color the lake black. The same water, just colored black with food coloring. Since then, not one visitor dared to even touch the water. Never underestimate the psychological power of color.

Deep Dive:
"Universal Principles of Design" by William Lidwell, Kritina Holden, Jill Butler

---

47 I have no idea who it was but for the story's sake, let's say it was a wise elder of the village. Perhaps a retired graphic designer.

70
Read the Opposite of What You Believe

Do you have strong beliefs? Great! Now test them. Read something that's the direct opposite of what you believe in. Why? If we read content just to confirm our thoughts and ideas, then we're only living in an echo chamber. And at this point, we have fallen fall the oldest trick in the book and that's the ol' "confirmation bias" trick.

If you don't know already, confirmation bias is the tendency to favor evidence that will support our already established argument and to ignore evidence that might refute it. Social media is notorious for feeding into this bias. Their algorithms learn what we like or dislike and supply us with more of what keeps us engaged. But you already knew that, right?

Don't fall in love with your thoughts and ideas. They're just thoughts and ideas are common. If they're any good, they should stand up to questioning and scrutiny.

Are you a socialist? Great! Maybe read something by Milton Friedman and Adam Smith. Are you an unapologetic capitalist? Awesome! Now read Karl Marx or Frederich Engels. Whatever you feel strongly about, put them to the test.

Shadow Someone for the Day

IF YOU EVER HAVE the opportunity to do this, I highly recommend it[48]. How else are you going to know what it's like to be a (fill in the blank of any profession you were curious about)?

I did this a few times; once with a friend who fixed copiers in downtown Boston and another who sold framed pictures door to door. What did it teach me? How hard it was to fix copiers and to sell art door to door! I quickly developed an appreciation for what I do now and a newfound respect for many that really have hard jobs.

---

48 And getting this opportunity is just a matter of asking someone.

72

Don't Try to be Everything to Everyone

As marketing genius, Seth Godin would say,

> *"If you are trying to be everything to everyone, you end up being nothing to no one."*

And...

> *"The riches are in the niches"*

It's tempting to cast a broad net and it makes some sense. If you're trying to market something, more people seemingly means more possibilities and potentially more sales. This might work on paper but it actually doesn't in the real world.

When you cast a very wide net, you're making an effort in reaching out to people that are not your tribe. And what that means is, when you're showing a product to someone that is not interested, you're wasting your valuable effort which can be very costly. In large niches, you also have far more competition and I will guarantee that you'll become invisible. This is one of the reasons why people that get excited about selling online eventually get discouraged.

Embrace your uniqueness and don't waste your efforts competing with the masses.

Deep Dive:
"Blue Oceans" by W. Chan Kim, Renée Mauborgne

73

Live Within Your Means but don't be a Martyr

We all want to pay off our debts, save for a house and hopefully retire. What if I told you that you can do all these adulting things and NOT penny-pinch? You want your money management to be sustainable. Suffering will just cause you to burn out and quit[49].

The trick is to find a sustainable way to enjoy life and save for your goals. Ramit Sethi, the author of, "I Will Teach You To Be Rich" suggests that we plan our spending. It's worthwhile to take the time and make a plan for the month. What sources of income do you have and where are they all going to go; savings, monthly bills, your Roth IRA, investments, food, etc. I'm not telling you anything new and you're probably thinking to yourself, 'Uh yeah, it's called a budget, duh!' But there's a caveat Sethi mentions in his book I like.

Along with your monthly expenses, set aside a certain percentage for your entertainment. Set up a separate checking account with your bank[50] and automatically withdraw your chosen amount for the month from your main account to your new FUN-D MONEY account. Yes, pun intended.

This is money you can spend for the month completely guilt-free. Want to buy expensive lattes at that fancy cafe'? No problem. Like getting drinks at a club on the weekend? Go for it! This is your reward for getting shit done. But if you decide to go crazy and blow all of your fun money on one weekend, we'll guess who's staying home for the rest of the month. So

---

49 One of the reasons why gyms are crowded in January and empty in February.
50 Most banks suck. Why not a credit union?

definitely set aside some fun guilt-free spending money along with all your other expenses. But it's up to you to make it last.

Deep Dive:
"I Will Teach You To Be Rich" by Ramit Sethi

74

Don't Get Eaten by Sharks

THIS IS THE BEST ADVICE I have given so far! But what does this have to do with art or design? I'll get to that in a second but first I want to overstate the obvious by starting the second paragraph with a simple, declarative sentence.

Nature is incredibly intelligent and adaptable. If you're not the strongest creature on the block, you could always look like one and pretend that you are. Or maybe camouflage your way into not being easily seen. But if you're a badass venomous sea snake[51] there's no reason to hide or pretend. Their black and white stripes mean I'm here, I mean business and I don't care who sees me.

Now we have to admit that sharks are pretty badass creatures in their own right. There are not many things sharks are afraid of with the exception of that scary sea snake. Sharks don't want anything to do with them and who can blame them?

Here's some good news for all you designers. Great design is all around us. Maybe we take it for granted and maybe not. Hopefully not, because lots of great ideas came from simple observation of nature's many wonders. Now with that said, let's get back to the snake and the shark.

Did I mention that in nature you don't have to be the biggest and the baddest on the block? One method of trickery in nature is called mimicry. Mimicry is simply copying what already exists with the hope that you will also inherit the benefits of the very thing you're mimicking. Case in point, the black and white stripes from those pesky, scary, sea snakes. Wearing black

---

[51] *I just hate the idea that venomous snakes are roaming free in the sea.*

and white striped swim and scuba suits are great shark deterrents! Apparently sharks least favorite color pattern.

Mother nature is an awesome designer. And she had millions of years to figure shit out. We can't go wrong in listening, seeing, and understanding how nature works. What other designs are going to be inspired simply from observing what nature has already mastered?

Happiness According to a Greek Philosopher

BEHOLD EPICURUS, just another ancient Greek philosopher. And what does he have to say for himself? Just the formula to happiness that's all.

Apparently, the formula isn't that complicated. According to Epicurus, there are only three ingredients needed for a happy life. Yep, just three but the catch is, you gotta have all three. Here they are:

The Three Components to Happiness:

1. **Friendship** - having healthy and close relations with people you love. Having people to share your life with.

2. **Freedom** - This is also known as autonomy, having the freedom to control what you do and how you do it. People that have this said autonomy at their job are far more satisfied with their job.

3. **Time** - Not just time itself but time for ourselves. Time for introspection and contemplation. Time to chill, relax and just be in the present moment.

Now, this might not be the formula that will cure everyone's unhappiness, but it's a good start. Notice how money isn't one of these?

Reference:
Epicurus on Happiness - Philosophy: A Guide to Happiness
https://www.youtube.com/watch?v=irornIAQzQY

76
Do Hard Things

IF SOMETHING WAS easy it would be boring. If something was too difficult to do, it would be frustrating. Challenge yourself to take on something just outside your comfort zone. Through these actions is how we progress.

We easily get confused about what we want out of life and what would make us happy. Case in point, what if you were given 10 million dollars? Easy! Hello, Caribbean beach and an endless supply of margaritas! Sure that would be fun, at least for a little while but really for how long? Wouldn't you get bored? Wouldn't you get restless?

It sounds counterintuitive but we like problems. Without them, life would be well not life at all! From challenges comes learning, growing, strength, and then ultimately purpose and happiness. Maybe the secret is to not try to remove all problems from your life but to lean into becoming and enjoying the act of problem-solving.

What I'm trying to say is, get comfortable with being uncomfortable. It's how gym rats learn to enjoy the feeling of being sore.

What We Overestimate and Underestimate

"Most people overestimate what they can do in one year and underestimate what they can do in ten years."
— Bill Gates

In general, we have a bias when it comes to time. We easily think we can do a lot in a small amount of time[52] but completely underestimate what we can achieve in the long term. This is why setting up small but consistent habits that benefit us daily adds up tremendously in the long term. Consistent investing over long periods and allowing the strength of compounding to work its magic is just one example of what we can achieve over a long period.

This is why I am a big fan of doing tiny habits. Will doing 20 pushups every morning for a few days get you in shape? Absolutely not. For a year, now we're talkin. Will smoking one cigarette kill you. Nope. How about smoking for 20 years. You're pushing your luck. Small habits, whether they are good or bad, may seem innocuous in the short term but over time, have monumental results.

---

52 *Have you ever finished your things-to-do list for the day? Exactly.*

Learn how to Brainstorm

WE HAVE ALL HEARD the term but do we really do it well, if at all? If you don't know the difference between convergent vs divergent thinking, then you could probably use a crash course in the art of brainstorming.

Divergent vs Convergent Thinking
Divergent (di meaning divide) means taking a thought or an idea and having another thought or idea branch from it. This is the creative process of thinking and is the heart and soul of the brainstorming session. It's also very important to hold any judgment of any contributions during this process. This is a non-judgment zone and sometimes silly and terrible ideas are encouraged to get the ball rolling.

Convergent (con meaning coming together) is the more logical part of the process and comes after the Divergent session. Here we're putting our judgment hat on and picking out the best and more practical ideas from our divergent thinking phase.

The trick is[53] to keep these two modes of thinking completely separate. Many a time we combine our divergent with our convergent and unlike peanut butter and chocolate, they don't go well together.

Here's a little tip on your next brainstorming session to keep the pesky convergent dominant brains at bay. When you're brainstorming with a group,

---

[53] *And this is where people commonly get brainstorming wrong. All too often, the divergent and the convergent modes are mixed into one session.*

here's a new rule. No one can ever say the word "no." If someone wants to add or think they have a better idea, they have to preclude it with a resounding "yes! and...." This way no one is feeling shut down, which is the main problem with convergent only brainstorming.

79

Solve the Right Problem

BEFORE YOU EMBARK on a challenging journey to solve a very difficult problem, first ask yourself, is this the right problem to solve?

In Rory Sutherland's book "Alchemy," the author points out a particularly common problem in English cities. Commuters don't like to take the train. So if you were to ask a commuter in England, what should be done to improve the transportation system, the common answer would be to make the daily trips shorter. If you looked at this problem from an engineer's perspective, the solution is simple: shorter trips mean making faster trains. But that would cost an enormous amount of taxpayer money and they're limits to how fast trains can go safely.

Is this solving the right problem? To Sutherland, absolutely not. The problem isn't the amount of time spent on the train, it's that commuters don't find commuting enjoyable. What would be the proper solution? Finding ways to make commuting more comfortable and enjoyable of course. There are far more possibilities in solving that problem and not to mention, much cheaper rather than trying to make faster trains.

Framing the problem from a different perspective could save a lot of money, frustration, time, and energy.

Deep Dive:
"Alchemy" by Rory Sutherland

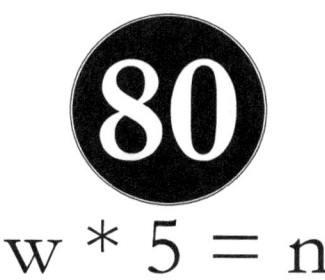

w * 5 = n

SPEAKING OF RIGHT ANSWERS, not only is asking the right questions important but also the amount of right questions matters. Let's take a look at a method of asking that will reveal these elusive answers.

Here's a real-world example, an incident that happened at an Amazon Fulfillment Center.

An Amazon employee injured his hand after trying to rescue his coat that he left on a conveyor belt that was suddenly turned on. Now it's easy to say that the problem is with the employee. He shouldn't be putting his things on active conveyor belts. But to get to the heart of the problem, we need to dig deeper.

Question 1: Why did the employee hurt his hand?
Answer 1: He put his coat on the conveyor belt.

Question 2: Why did he put his coat on the conveyor belt?
Answer 2: He needed a place to put it while he was getting ready to leave.

Question 3: Why did he not have a place to put his things?
Answer 3: Because there isn't enough room for employees' things.

Question 4: Why isn't there enough room?
Answer 4: Because we just hired a lot of new employees and don't have enough lockers and coat hooks for everyone.

Question 5: Why don't we have enough coat hooks?
Answer 5: We neglected to order enough lockers for the new employees.

BINGO.

The real solution to the problem isn't to scold employees for putting their things where they don't belong, It's to find out why they're doing it in the first place.

81
Learn to Stress Out

Is stress really that bad for us? The answer surprisingly is not a hard yes. According to health psychologist Kelly McGonigal, it all comes down to mindset[54].

As a disclaimer, she agrees that chronic stress is always bad. It causes inflammation and therefore all kinds of disease. But when we're dealing with everyday stress, is it the actual stress or is it how we react to stress? McGonigal says, let's not try to get rid of stress, let's get better at stress. Instead of reducing stress, we should practice stress resilience; "How you think and how you act can transform your experience of stress."

Interestingly, our mindset on stress may dictate how stress can manifest itself biologically. So the next time if you are feeling nervous, switch it to, "I'm feeling excited!" Because it's true, you are excited (masked as a negative sensation we labeled as stress) and it's perfectly normal and OK to feel that way.

There are so many things to unpack here one can't possibly do it justice just on one page. If you do suffer from anxiety, please please please read this book. There's also a very popular TED talk she did years ago. The link is below.

Deep Dive:
"The Upside of Stress" by Kelly McGonigal

---

54 Have I mentioned that mindset is everything?

82

To Resolute or not Resolute?

At the beginning of every year, we follow the same tradition. Resolve to become a better person. And what's so wrong with that? Nothing. It's a noble endeavor. The problem is that we only do it once a year where we should be doing it every day.

I mean it, every day. I'm going to refer back to Robert Allen's book, "The Four Maps of Happy Successful People" which reminds us that our brains love patterns of behavior[55]. Brains like patterns because patterns are easy to execute and don't require a lot of energy. Patterns make us run on autopilot. Good patterns serve us. When we make a resolution, we are attempting to break a bad pattern by making another at the beginning of the year. Deep down we know it's going to take more than that, so much more.

What Allen suggests in his book is to constantly remind ourselves of our goals; our 5 year, 1 year, 1-month goals, and one-day goals. And it's all because our brains are great forgetting machines. Yes, our brains do love patterns, but to install a new positive pattern, we have to continuously remind it. This is where vision boards and affirmations come into play. It's not that you're miraculously manifesting your reality when you see a visionboard or read an affirmation[56], rather it's a simple and constant reminder to yourself what's important and why you're working so hard.

---

55 Also known as habits but let's call them patterns here.
56 Hell maybe you are! I'm not going to rule out anything.

Deep Dive:
"The Four Maps of Happy Successful People" by Robert Allen

83

Give Credit Where Credit's Due

I BELIEVE THERE are rules that artists ought to live by. When I was a kid, tracing a drawing was out of the question. That was cheating! How well you can draw "freehand" was a mark of a talented artist. But here's a rule we all should embrace and be equally as stringent with: giving other creators full attribution for their work.

According to Austin Kleon, author of "Share Your Work" and Steal Like an Artist," we're a bit lazy when it comes to the attribution front. When sharing other artist's work, Kleon suggests we think of asking ourselves, "...what the work is, who made it, how they made it, when and where it was made, why you're sharing it, why people should care about it, and where people can see some more work like it. Attribution is about putting little museum labels next to the stuff you share."

Also, according to Austin, we tend to neglect where we found the content. "It's always good practice to give a shout-out to the people who have helped you stumble onto good work.." Austin states.

You can always put your own spin on a concept, but don't pretend that the original concepts were your own inventions. If we're the one doing the sharing; whether it be artwork or an idea, we should give credit where credit's due. Sharing is caring.

Deep Dive:
"Credit is Always Due" by Austin Kleon
https://austinkleon.com/2014/01/27/credit-is-always-due/

84

The War of Art

"IF YOU FIND YOURSELF asking, 'Am I really a writer? Am I really an artist?' chances are you are. The counterfeit innovator is wildly self-confident. The real one is scared to death."
— Steven Pressfield

Does something you want to do also gives you fear and anxiety? Good! This is known as what Pressfield calls *resistance*. Resistance will come in the form of self-doubt, distraction, fear, anything to derail us from the very thing we ought to be doing. And remember if it's hard to do, it's probably worth doing. If you have ever felt this, this book seems to be tailored for you.

Procrastination. Why do we do it? Fear. And it's sooo bloody natural to have this fear which is why it's sooo bloody common. Here's the antidote. Forgive yourself for sucking but just don't forgive, give ample amount of space for sucking. Perhaps our old fixed mindsets[57] behind the scenes are still telling us that we have to be great always, even if we're starting something new. Don't listen. We get better through the process so the sooner you start sucking the better you'll become. Embrace the suck.

Deep Dive:
"The War of Art: Break Through the Blocks & Win Your Inner Creative Battles" by Steven Pressfield

---

57 Remember Chapter 12 about the difference between a growth and a fixed mindset.

85
Don't Wait for Inspiration

THE MOST COMMON MISTAKE we artists do is to wait until they are in the mood before starting a project. It's like waiting for some muse to anoint us from above to move forward and allow us to make something worth making. The issue we have is actually inverted. What we need to do is get in motion and start something, anything and the inspiration and motivation will follow.

"I write only when inspiration strikes. Fortunately, it strikes every morning at nine o'clock sharp."
— Somerset Maugham

Here's another myth to bust wide open. There is no such thing as writer's block. Sorry, there just isn't. Just as there's no such thing as plumber's block, carpenter's block, or dental hygienist block. Our so-called blocks are us thinking everything coming from our hands has to be great. It would serve us to abandon this perfectionist mindset. Perfectionism is just a sneaky disguise for procrastination. And if we're procrastinating from doing the things we need to do to move forward, then we have to dig deep, really deep, and figure out why. Is it fear of failure? Or success? Or just your way of self-sabotage? If you can dig deep, you can uncover what your subconscious is holding onto and keeping you from moving forward.

In the meantime, make terrible art, terrible writing, terrible music, or terrible anything. Because the great eventually comes through the process.

Deep Dive:
"How to Fail at Almost Everything and Still Win Big" by Scott Adams

The Spirit of the Amateur

THE WORD AMATEUR doesn't have a positive ring to it. But what's the true definition of amateur? Amateur: "...from French amateur "one who loves, lover" (16c., restored from Old French ameour), from Latin amatorem (nominative amator) "lover, friend," agent noun from amatus, past participle of amare "to love."

Sure, we all want to aim for being professionals. Professionals are supposed to be good at their craft, so good that they get to charge money for it. But amateurs do it for the love of it. They may or may not be good at it, but they enjoy it and that's something to respect.

Sometimes we get so big for our britches we forget the whole reason why we got into this crazy field to begin with. Let's not take ourselves too seriously and now and then, embrace our inner amateur selves.

Deep Dive:
The Definition of Amateur
https://www.etymonline.com/search?q=amateur

87

Redefine Wealth

SINCE WE'RE ON AN etymology kick, let's take look at the word wealth.

Wealth: Word that came from the 13th century and it originally meant, "happiness, well being, health and including prosperity of possessions or riches."

What can this tell us? There are more facets to wealth than what's in your bank account. A fat bank account is great[58] but according to wealth, it literally isn't everything.

While serving in the Peace Corps in Jamaica, I witnessed incredible poverty. Now did that condition cause them stress and did they want to change their status? Of course. Yet I haven't witnessed the loneliness, depression, anxiety, and anger in what seems to be an epidemic in the States. Wealth like intelligence comes in many forms and should be approached holistically.

Deep Dive:
"The Money Maven"
https://patricewashington.com

The Definition of Wealth
https://www.etymonline.com/search?q=wealth

---

58 And one day I would like to have one of those fat bank accounts!

Get Over Your Hangups with Money

Do you have hangups when it comes to money? Probably. I know I have, but I'm now conscious of them and working on developing more positive mindsets when it comes to money. Here are a few money tropes I had brewing in my subconscious:

- Money is the root of all evil
- Having too much money is selfish
- Rich people are greedy
- Poverty is virtuous
- If I had more money than my friends, they won't like me for me, they will only like me for the money I have. Or perhaps hate me!
- Being rich is sinful and immoral

The first one on the list, "Money is the root to all evil" was a big one for me to get over. And I'm happy to say that it no longer resonates with me. What did I replace it with? New healthy mindset: 1) You cannot give what you do not have to take care of yourself first. 2) Wealthy people are not necessarily greedy and evil and poor people are not inherently virtuous. 3) Money is nothing more than energy and energy was meant to move. Having this energy gives you the power to help people around you and the world.

Your external world is a mirror of your internal world. Remember that thoughts and ideas are things and they become powerful things when they are believed. If I haven't said it before, test everything you think and believe, especially if you inherited them. Your beliefs on money could be the very thing that's holding you back.

Exercise:

What are your hangups with money? What belief systems have you inherited that you should be questioning? Write them down and seriously question whether they are true or not.

Second, write down 5 positives about money. How could having more money in your life help you, the people around you, and help you live a more fulfilled life?

If you're ready to seriously test your beliefs around money, I highly suggest Jen Sincero's book, "You Are a Badass at Making Money"

Deep Dive:
   "You Are a Badass at Making Money" by Jen Sincero

Charismatic Lives Matter

LIKE I MENTIONED BEFORE, your work doesn't speak for itself, you have to speak up for it. Like it or not, people are judging you; the way you walk, talk, and how you carry yourself.

Now if you're OK with deliberately not caring about what others think of you,[59] that's fine. But these judgments that society makes on us have a direct impact on our lives. How we carry ourselves through life, how we speak, how we walk, our posture, our mannerisms, you name it has an impact on our jobs and in our relationships. This happens whether we like it or not.

So there's something to be said about this thing called charisma. Charisma isn't something you're born with, it's something you learn how to do. Charisma is a skill just like any other, you practice to get better at it. And the good news is that there are plenty of exercises to practice to hone our charisma skills. Check out the link below. There are videos that show how you can get started on being more charismatic. Also, if you're looking for a deeper dive, check out the book, "Captivate by Vanessa Van Edwards.

Deep Dive::
"Charisma on Command"
https://www.youtube.com/c/Charismaoncommand

"Captivate" by Vanessa Van Edwards

---

59 Chances are you do. We all do. It's part of being a social creature.

90

No One is Coming to Save You

YEARS AGO, I HAD a health crisis. It was nothing major but at the time I thought it was[60]. I was getting dizzy spells, couldn't think straight and my hair was falling out. However my doctor was far more relaxed about it than I was. He said, "your blood test tells us that you have hypothyroidism.

'Um, Thyroid? What the hell is a thyroid and why is mine hypo?' These were the thoughts I had. "Ah don't worry, it's an easy fix." The doctor said. "Just take these pills[61] for the rest of your life."

And so I did and for a while, I felt better. Much better. Until I didn't. I went back to my doctor to up my meds, assuming that would be an easy fix.

"Hmmm. Your latest blood test tells me you're in the normal range[62] so there isn't any reason to increase your medication." I was devastated. The person I relied on for my well-being was my doctor and he couldn't help me even when it seemed that the solution was so easy.

I realized that no one was coming to "save me." So I did what I should have done a long time ago; take responsibility for my own well-being. I immediately quit smoking (cold turkey style!), started eating healthy, got in tune

---

60 I was a smoker then and if anything came up health-wise, I immediately thought cancer, tumor, death!
61 A common supplement for this condition is Synthroid and it's a substitute for natural thyroid hormone.
62 By the way, that's a very large range!

with nature, started working out like a gym rat, and most of all, DETOXED DETOXED DETOXED! It didn't happen overnight but today I'm feeling so much better than I ever have. All this without having to up my supplements every 6 months.

And although I wouldn't wish this on anyone, this disease[63] taught me a lesson. I needed to take responsibility for my well-being. Doctors are great but they don't know everything and some of them, unfortunately, don't have your best interests in mind. I decided to educate myself. I wasn't asking for anyone's permission and I certainly wasn't going to wait to be rescued by someone with a degree and a white coat.

Going beyond my physical health, I began to take more responsibility for other areas in my life as well. In retrospect, I was transitioning from a disempowering victim's mindset, to what's known as a survival mindset; a mindset that embraces tenacity, resilience, and your ability to adapt and grow.

It's the challenges in our lives that can ultimately make us stronger.

Deep Dive:
Anything by David Goggins but you're forewarned, Goggins takes personal responsibility to an extreme. I am not kidding at all.

---

63 Technically it's called Hashimoto's disease and it's an autoimmune disease. A pretty common one, unfortunately. If you're having symptoms, I highly suggest that you get a blood test to check your levels. Keep in mind that other factors can cause your thyroid to under perform so don't assume it's Hashimoto's. To make sure, request that you take an antibody test.

91

The World Doesn't Owe You Anything

I THINK IT'S EASY, especially within our culture, to develop a sense of entitlement. It's as if the world owes us the life we desire and all the goodness it has to offer. Actually, all that might be true. We may be worthy of all the goodness in the world but let me tell ya, nothing ain't free. It's our duty to work towards this goodness. And the goodness will be sweeter, knowing right well that we earned every bit of it. We may live in an abundant and infinite universe, but we have to meet the universe halfway.

> *"Don't believe the world owes you a living. The world owes you nothing. It was here first."*
>
> — Robert J. Burdette

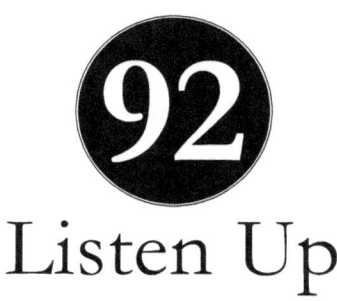

Listen Up

"LISTEN WITH CURIOSITY. Speak with honesty. Act with integrity. The greatest problem with communication is we don't listen to understand. We listen to reply. When we listen with curiosity, we don't listen with the intent to reply. We listen for what's behind the words."

— Roy T. Bennett, The Light in the Heart

YOU ALREADY KNOW that listening is an important skill to have and vital for relationships. We all want to be heard right? Here's an area where we think we're good at but probably not. Well, I have learned, and now passing it on to you, that there are two types of listening: active and passive listening.

Passive listening is the most common. This type of listening allows the other speaker to talk with a minimal amount of engagement from the listener. The listener is either distracted, tuned out, or thinking about how to respond. Either way, they are not fully engaged, and often, the speaker can pick up on it. Unfortunately, we're all guilty of it and have, at one time or another, been the recipient of it as well.

Active listening.

The complete opposite of passive listening, active listening is when the listener is fully engaged, reading the speaker's verbal and non-verbal cues. Active listeners have removed all distractions like phones, are fully attentive to the speaker and use small utterances to reassure the speaker that they are being heard. Active listening allows the speaker to fully speak while you're fully engaged.

What Active Listening is Not.

Active is not thinking and rehearsing what to say before we say it. It's not interrupting with your thoughts or counterarguments and it's not being constantly distracted by environmental factors[64].

Good listening is a skill and like anything you want to get better at you have to practice. Within our ever-increasing distracted world, we've developed some bad habits. To break these will take some effort, especially when it comes to distractions. So practice your concentration and resist the urge to check your phone – even if it's just for 10 minutes– when someone is talking to you.

Deep Dive:
   "Active Listening: Hear What People Are Really Saying"
   https://www.mindtools.com/CommSkll/ActiveListening.htm

   "Active Listening Skills" by Communication Coach Alex Lyon
   https://www.youtube.com/watch?v=7wUCyjiyXdg

---

64 Sure, you may have put the phone away, but your distracted tendencies still exist.

93
Become Worth Following

IF YOU'RE PERSISTENT on becoming a professional artist, you're at some point are going to try try try your darnedest to promote your art on all social media platforms.

Please don't take it from me, I'm still trying to figure out all the socials. But what I do know and what has been validated by far more successful artists than myself, is this; be worth following. What does that mean? It means spending the time and giving quality content that has value for others. Think about what you would follow. Most likely it's giving you value in one way or another. It's simple. I didn't say easy, just simple. Know your audience and create value for that audience.

The Futur

I like to reference these guys a lot because they are doing so many things right. In this case, they have a great Instagram account and have really mastered the art of carousels. If you don't know, carousels is an Instagram post where you can compile multiple images together into one post. What the Futur decided to do is turn these carousel posts into mini art lessons. Brilliant! So far they are worked out in their favor and they work simply because they are giving little nuggets of value for free to their audience.

94

Distraction or Traction

I LOVE LISTS! Strange I know. Especially Things-To-Do lists. I'm rather forgetful so writing a list is a perfect solution. Or is it?

Actually, a things-to-do list is a great distraction tool in a clever disguise. It's masked as a productivity tool but this very tool could be keeping us from doing the very things we need to do. And that's the hard work. The work that matters. The work that would move the needle for us if we could just stay focused.

Try this instead. Keep your beloved things-to-do list[65] but consider only writing down 3 main items. That's it, three. Just three important items that if got done, would make the day a smashing success. Think about what three things you need to do to make this day truly count. Write them down and commit to yourself that you'll get these done.

---

65 *Perhaps demote the list by calling it Tasks or Errands.*

95
Learned Helplessness

Take two groups of dogs. Put both groups in separate cages. Group one gets an electric shock[66] if they try to escape. Group two doesn't get shocked and escapes easily. Now take the two groups and put them into the same cages. There are no shocks. Group two, as predicted, easily escapes but group one doesn't even try. Those poor group one dogs learned helplessness.

We can easily learn helplessness from beliefs developed from our past failures[67]. Like the electric shocks, our own past experiences may feel very real and were based on a past truth. But if there's one thing you can take away from this lil book, it's this: THE PAST DOES NOT EQUAL THE FUTURE. Continuing to believe that the past does equal the future is under minding your abilities, which can become self-fulfilling.

Deep Dive:
"Learned Optimism" by Martin Seligman

---

66 I know, savages, right? Keep in mind that this was the 60's. I don't think we could get away with shocking dogs these days nor should we!
67 Our personal electric shocks

Are Pictures are Better Than Words?

SORRY WORDSMITHS, BUT there are some important advantages visual images have over the written word.

A case for symbols. It comes down to how our brains work. An image simply takes less effort to process than words and they're easier to recall. A string of words can be processed quickly, but it takes significant focus and energy, which our brains are always trying to conserve.

Are pictures better than words? Well, it's not a simple yes and no. Symbols make processing and understanding quick and easy. But let's not throw out the written word altogether. Using a combination of words and images is a powerful one-two punch. According to the study (Link below) "we store visual and verbal memories separately." So if it's your goal to have someone remember something important, it's best to link your text with an image. Peoples' memories will make a strong connection.

Let's just say that we're all visual learners.

Deep Dive:
"Words Versus Pictures: Leveraging the Research on Visual Communication"
https://journal.lib.uoguelph.ca

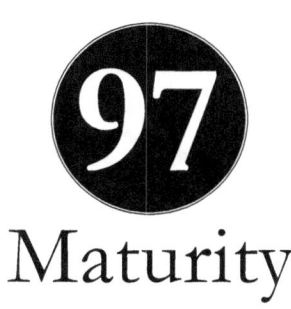

Maturity

HAVE YOU EVER BEEN embarrassed by your past behaviors? Good. Do you cringe at what you said or behaved 10 years ago? Five years ago? Maybe even last year!? Awesome! That's a good sign you're heading in the right direction and it's called maturity.

Maturity is an indicator that we're simply becoming better people, better versions of ourselves. So if you're embarrassed at the things you did when you were younger. Congratulations! So far your adulting well!

Although there is usually a parallel, age is not always a good indicator of maturity. Maturity is less about how old someone is and more about how you see, behave and approach the world. To label someone as immature is to say, they don't have a good grasp on the world, how to interact with others and how to respond appropriately.

My top 5 signs that you are becoming mature:

- You make peace with realizing that you don't know everything and you don't have all the answers and it's OK. You embrace humility.
- You develop more empathy and compassion for others. You become kinder and more selfless.
- You ditch your rigidity and lean more on flexibility and openness. You're more accepting of other points of view without the need to react.
- You ditch your rude, impulsive and, irrational behavior for good manners and a sense of calm.
- Take responsibility for everything in your life.

The Marshmallow Test

HERE'S A FUN EXERCISE that involves design, team building, and marshmallows. You will need 4 teams of 4 people and give them these materials[68]:

- 20 sticks of spaghetti
- 1 yard of tape
- 1 yard of string
- 1 marshmallow

Here's the objective. See what team can build the tallest structure in 20 minutes. And here's the challenge. The marshmallow has to be on top. Sounds simple but simple doesn't equate to easy.

The creator of this challenge, Peter Skillman, brought together teams based on their profession. These teams were business graduates, lawyers, CEOs, and kindergartners. And yes, if you guessed it, the kindergartners were the most successful.

How could little kids beat professional adults? The challenge exposed how we, as adults, act within groups. What do we typically do? We spend a lot of time planning, analyzing, organizing, thinking, creating political hierarchies, and establishing authority within the group. In the meantime, the kids jumped right into testing and prototyping. Another aspect that separated the adults from the kindergarten champs was that the adults placed the marshmallow last, creating a lot of 'whew!' or 'Oh f**k!' moments. Since the objective was to create a structure that supports a weighty object, the kids always started with the marshmallow.

---

68 This is if you want to do this professionally, but it sounds like fun just with an informal group of friends!

So what's the takeaway on this one. Adults suck! LOL. As adults, we fell in love with organizing and planning and thinking something to death when we should have just played. We as adults, with our titles and egos, hate hate hate to be wrong. So we plan, over plan, and waste time thinking about our over planning. Kids have no such issues with being wrong. They didn't waste time trying and failing over and over again. In fact, the kindergartners got 4-5 times more chances by starting early compared to the adults who had a one-and-done chance with the marshmallow.

Fear of failing can pressure us to not start and to overthink, over research, and over plan. We have forgotten or perhaps never have known that failing is a part of the process. So go ahead and fail, but fail first, fail often, and fail quickly. The good stuff is just past our failures.

Learn How to See, Learn How to Speak

So you probably know that people buy from people they like. They also buy from people that know what they're talking about. To become an expert in our field, we got to be able to talk the talk[69].

Art courses have introduced this to us in the form of a critique. Saying something is "good" isn't, well good enough. As artists, we need to hone in on the language of art. We can't just say something is "good", we need to go into detail about why this said something is good.

I love the exercise Chris Do from The Futur[70] runs though in a webinar (link to the webinar is below). In the exercise, Chris asks the participants to pick a work of art. For his example, he shows us a painting his son painted in the style of Jean-Michel Basquiat. Here's the challenge, articulate what makes a Basquiat painting a Basquiat. Is it the shapes, the colors, the brush strokes, the subject matter, the perspective? This challenge forces you to think and articulate the essence of the art before you. It's not always easy, but it's a good challenge and worth getting good at.

Deep Dive:
"How To Learn From Any Piece of Art (5 Ingredients Breakdown)"
www.youtube.com/watch?v=l4KnDY-HUxQ

---

69 And no, I definitely don't mean bullshit.
70 Yes! Another "The Futur" reference!

Get to the Next Barrel

STARTING SOMETHING BIG is daunting. Writing a book, painting a mural, creating a website[71]. Most of us procrastinate because of this, "dauntiness." But remember, anything that's worthwhile doing is going to have its challenges. So when things seem overwhelming, think about this real-life scenario that Brian Tracy calls, "Getting to your Next Barrel."

Getting to your Next Barrel
Crossing a huge desert like the Sahara is a daunting task. Many have gotten lost and many have died. To help travelers cross more safely, the French marked the track with black oil barrels. These barrels were placed 5 kilometers apart; just close enough to keep the one you left and the one in front of you within sight. So instead of having a whole desert to cross at once, all you have to do now is get to the next barrel.

Keep this in mind when you're starting any large project. Get your mind off of the big picture and take one single action forward, to your next barrel.

Deep Dive:
  "Eat That Frog!" by Brian Tracey

---
71 *Hell, even painting your kitchen cabinets is a massive project. I would know.*

Becoming a Master

DID YOU KNOW THERE are different levels to reading?[72] The top reading level, the one that is right there on top of the food chain of reading, is known as synoptical reading.

Synoptical reading is not reading to understand the book, it's to understand the subject the book is based on. This type of reading is more involved and it takes reading multiple books on the same subject and comparing them.

If you want to become an expert in a field, read multiple books on the same subject and try to find a wide range of different perspectives. For example, if you wanted to get a good handle on economics, start with Milton Freidman AND Karl Marx[73]. You couldn't get more different from that!

Many times we search out content that we already agree with, reaffirming our confirmation bias. Again, this is something we want to steer away from. Your goal is to develop your own opinion, what is known as an "informed opinion." This is based on research, an observance of different points of view, and plenty of time to mull it all over.

You'll also need to take your opinion on the subject and bring that to the test. This will come when you reach out for different perspectives that you would have earlier dismissed. You don't have to agree, but collecting multiple perspectives on a subject will help you form your own position.

Deep Dive:
  "How to Read a Book" by Mortimer J. Adler

---

[72] *Actually, there are five.*
[73] *Yeah I know, I already made this analogy before...*

Conclusion

WELL THAT'S ALL I GOT FOR YOU. I'm hoping that you got at least a little something out of this book but actually I'm hoping you got a lot more than a little something. Optimally, you got a lotta somethings which, of course, would be great. Granted, it wasn't a long book or even a difficult one to read. But sometimes good things come in small packages. This was a small package.

If there was something I missed, got wrong, you disagreed with, or got you inspired to read more of, feel free to drop a message. You can reach me at:

zajacmark@yahoo.com

Also, please visit my silly lil publishing company at:

www. piggybackpress.com

Thank you for your support. I appreciate you and wish you all the best this crazy, mixed up world has got to offer.

Book References

Austin, Kleon (2014). Show your work.

Dweck, Carol (2006). Mindset: The new psychology of success.

Johnson, Spencer Dr. (1999). Who moved my cheese?

Sutherland, Rory (2019). Alchemy.

Newport, Carl (2016). Deep work.

Tracy, Brian (2001) Eat that frog!

Lidwell, William. Holden, Kritina. Butler, Jill. (2003). Universal principles of design.

Kiyosaki, Robert. (1997). Rich dad, poor dad. www.richdad.com

Allen, Robert. (2016) The four maps of happy successful people.

Seneca. On the shortness of life .

Adams, Scott. (2013). How to fail at almost everything and still win big.

Neumeier, Marty. (2006). Zag.

Sincero, Jen. (2017). You are a badass at making money.

Schwartz, Barry. (2005). The paradox of choice.

Chan Kim, W. Mauborgne, Renée. (1994) Blue ocean strategy.

Sethi, Ramit. (2009). I will teach you to be rich.

McGonigal, Kelly. (2015). The upside of stress.

Pressfield, Steven. (2003). The war of art.

Van Edwards, Vanessa. (2017) Captivate.

Seligman, Martin. (2006) Learned optimism.

Adler, Mortimer J. (1972) How to read a book.

Godin, Seth. (2018). This is Marketing.

If you would like to purchase any of these books or just plain curious about them, you can get easy access to them by going to: piggybackpress/ life-after-art school.

Biography

Mark Zajac is currently a graphic designer, illustrator, and a 'sometimes' artist and muralist for wealthy people. With the help of a lot of coffee, he occasionally puts groups of words together with the hope that it will inspire, motivate and make sense to someone other than himself.

www.ingramcontent.com/pod-product-compliance
Lightning Source LLC
Chambersburg PA
CBHW052349220526
45465CB00003BA/1021